ARCHITECTURAL
WORKING
DRAWINGS

MARVIN L. THOMAS, AIA

ARCHITECTURAL WORKING DRAWINGS

A Professional Technique

McGRAW-HILL BOOK COMPANY

New York   St. Louis   San Francisco   Auckland   Bogotá   Düsseldorf
Johannesburg   London   Madrid   Mexico   Montreal   New Delhi   Panama
Paris   São Paulo   Singapore   Sydney   Tokyo   Toronto

Library of Congress Cataloging in Publication Data

Thomas, Marvin L, date
Architectural working drawings.

Includes index.
1. Architectural drawing—Technique.   I.   Title.
NA2708.T46   720'.28   77-26084
ISBN 0-07-064240-0

1234567890   HAHA   7654321098

The editors for this book were Jeremy Robinson and Joseph
Williams, the designer was Elliot Epstein, and the production
supervisor was Frank Bellantoni. It was set in Helvetica by
University Graphics.

Printed and bound by Halliday Lithographics.

. . . to my wife Norma

CONTENTS

PREFACE

This book is designed to serve as:

1. A comprehensive professional technique for the development of architectural working drawings

2. A tabletop manual for draftors

3. A complete working drawing system for many offices and a reference format for those other offices that are interested in setting up an individual production system

4. An advanced training textbook for architectural students

5. A guide to self-criticism and self-improvement for draftors

6. An effective reference for mechanical, electrical, and structural engineers who regularly consult with architects and prepare drawings that must be coordinated with the architectural drawing system

7. An evaluation of photodrafting techniques

8. An introduction to the metric system

This book is not intended to be a primer on the subject of architectural drafting; it is written on the assumption that the reader has at least a working knowledge of the drawings required for building construction.

Professional offices vary in size and abilities, from the company with a sole architect who does everything to large organizations with multidisciplined teams that are assigned to various phases of a project; but all must produce working drawings of professional quality, coordinated with all the other disciplines. Working drawings are of necessity time-consuming and thus costly. Because of this, an efficient, industry-coordinated system of preparing working drawings would seem to be required, but few architectural (or engineering) offices can exhibit any disciplined or documented method for this fundamental work process. Because it would be unwieldy to attempt to separate the disciplines and functions necessary for each size and structure of office organization, this book is generally directed to the developing professional within an average size and type of architectural office. Such an office would have one or more principals producing working drawings for each project by means of draftors supervised by a project captain, utilizing the services of professional consultants for structural, mechanical, electrical, and other specialties. All this work is done under the general direction of a project architect.

Hard work alone does not produce excellent working drawings. There must also be (1) a fundamental knowledge of construction methods and materials and (2) a satisfactory drawing technique. Technique is (1) the ability to draw and to letter well and (2) a system by which this may be accomplished in a competent and expeditious manner. It is costly and time-consuming to experiment with a new system for each set of working drawings. It is far better to learn well and to follow a proven system—one that allows the personnel to be more efficient and more accurate and to better concentrate on the design conditions.

The standardization of working drawing techniques within each office is essential to production efficiency, coordination, and quality control. Standardization between offices and throughout the building construction industry is highly desirable and is entirely possible, but it has not been done, and it will not be accomplished suddenly. One of the major objectives of this book is to set forth practical principles and methods leading toward this standardization.

There are many benefits to be derived from a high degree of standardization. The builder can be assured that the intent, the abbreviations, the symbols, and the system of organization of the working drawings will be reasonably consistent among all design professionals. The architect can be assured that the intent and content of the office drawings are reasonably aligned with those of other offices, and as a result of not having to tailor the drawing methods to each project, the work force can better spend its time in design improvement and in quality control. Further, everyone benefits when students and draftors learn a basic system with techniques that need not be substantially varied from office to office.

Much of the material in this book is the result of compiling and evaluating known techniques. Some of the significant methods were originated by the author. All the techniques are time- and experience-tested in architectural practice. In the interest of presenting a unified system with a high degree of standardization, very few optional methods are mentioned. The resulting system is believed to be highly appropriate to and adequate for the preparation of drawings for most building projects. However, in any specific project there will be circumstances that will require special methods of drawing, scheduling, or notation to account for unusual conditions of the construction.

Some government agencies and some private owners have established standards for the drafting of documents for their projects. At times, some of the principles and techniques included in this book will be at variance, or even in contradiction, with such special standards. In those cases the owner's standards must be followed.

An introduction to the metric system is presented in Chapter 5 for the purpose of developing a general understanding of the measurement system that will soon be in general use in the building construction industry. This is not an attempt to present a complete treatise on metrics nor a development of the subject for engineering principles. In a few of the illustrations in this book, the metric equivalent will accompany the foot/inch dimension as a suggested method for showing both during the "transition period."

Drawings and specifications are legal documents, and since some of the methods suggested herein are not traditional, each reader/user must decide on the appropriate individual employment of these methods. Neither the author nor the publisher hereby assumes any legal obligation or liability for the use of any of the methods, suggestions, or data in this book. Occasionally, a manufacturer or a well-known trade name is used in the description of a product or article of equipment. This is only to assist in identifying a type of acceptable product or article and not to recommend or endorse it. In most cases, many satisfactory equivalents are available.

It is refreshing to see many women now engaged in architecture, traditionally a man's world. The term "architect" is complimentary to either gender, but the term "draftsman" now seems dated and discriminating. Therefore, this book addresses all those involved in drafting as *draftors*.

ACKNOWLEDGMENTS

Acknowledgment is made with grateful thanks for these efforts:

Assistance in editing the final manuscript:
Suzi Thomas McPherson, Great Bend, Ks.

Fast-Track and Construction Management:
Robert S. Slemmons, Topeka, Ks.
William Rinner, Topeka, Ks.

Photodrafting:
Donald Combs, Denver, Co.
L. K. Greene. Topeka, Ks.

Engineering Symbols:
George D. Majors, Lakewood, Co.

1

GENERAL
PURPOSE AND
PHILOSOPHY

1 | GENERAL PURPOSE AND PHILOSOPHY

THE OBJECTIVE OF WORKING DRAWINGS

Working drawings are a communication medium whose purpose is to graphically convey the design requirements for a construction project. They control the design by indicating the construction in considerable detail; if they are sufficiently detailed, a competent builder can construct the project in accordance with the design and without confusion. They are not *shop drawings* indicating every condition in exhaustive detail.

The drawings work cooperatively with the specifications. Together they illustrate and describe the intended results. Whatever is clearly indicated in either (by drawing, note, schedule, or description) is sufficient for a contract requirement. To repeat the requirement in both the drawings and the specifications is neither necessary nor desirable, and it increases the chances for errors and contradictions.

RESPONSIBILITY

In the production of working drawings, the draftor must assume a large measure of responsibility for accuracy and thoroughness and must not assume that a checker will discover every error and omission. Such errors and omissions are of serious concern, for they will certainly result in loss of time and money for someone— the architect, the owner, or the contractor—or for all of them. The work should be done as though the draftor's professional reputation were at stake; *it is*.

The drawings must illustrate only that which is certain. *Nothing should be assumed.* All related data must be thoroughly researched, and if there is doubt or if the necessary information cannot be promptly found, the supervisor should be consulted.

No drawing should be considered complete until the draftor has carefully compared it with the office's standard checklist and with the requirements for the specific project.

Changes in the drawings-in-progress are inevitable. When a

change is necessary, the draftor must make certain that every other drawing and specification thereby affected is changed accordingly—and immediately. The completed drawings are required to bear the seal of the architect-in-charge. The draftor must never apply the seal or release any drawing until the architect has thoroughly reviewed and approved it.

PRODUCTION TIME AND EXPENSE BUDGETING

The drawings required for two projects are seldom alike in scope and purpose. The quantity and complexity of the drawing details for a sophisticated private residence will obviously be different from those for a simple, project-type house, and different from those for a museum building. A difference in the drawings may also be required by the manner by which the project is to be constructed— by a bid contract, by a negotiated contract, by a project builder, by the Fast-Track system, or by the construction management process. At the very outset a realistic relationship must be established between the available fee and the type and quantity of drawings necessary to ensure good construction.

The responsibility for scheduling and time budgeting—thus profit or loss in the Working Drawings Phase—rests primarily with management. A carefully prepared schedule coordinating the dates of performance required by the office personnel, the consultants, and the owner, together with a realistic number of hours budgeted for the draftors, will serve as an effective performance yardstick. Figure 1-1 is an example of a project time and expense budget for a hypothetical project. In essence, this method deducts the extraneous expenses from the architectural fee to produce a net production fee, which, when divided by the average production-hour rate (including salaries, overhead, profit, etc.), will yield the total number of hours to be allocated for production. This hour limit is then assigned to the various production phases by percentages based on the office's time records of similar projects, resulting in

PROJECT TIME and EXPENSE BUDGET					
PROJECT *No Name Bank*				Date *8-9-78*	
ESTIMATED TOTAL ARCHITECTURAL FEES				$ *95,000*	
Less Consultant Fees:					
	Structural		$ *9,320*		
	Mechanical		$ *7,400*		
	Electrical		$ *4,780*		
	Interiors		$ *1,600*		
			$		
			$		
Less Direct Expenses (trips, model, rendering, and other			$ *2,500*		
Est. No. Trips *75*		Total Expenses		$ *25,600*	
		Net Production Fee		$ *69,400*	
Maximum Projected Hours by Phases					
Net Fee ÷ Avg. Production Hr. Rate @ $ *20.00*				*3,470* Tot. Hrs.	

Code	Phase	Personnel	Tot.Hrs.x %=		Max. Hrs.
C	Schematic (Concept)	Pro	*3470 x 10.0*		*347*
		Parapro	*8.5*		*295*
D	Design Development	Pro	*6.0*		*208*
		Parapro	*4.0*		*139*
W	Working Drawings	Pro	*17.0*		*590*
		Parapro	*20.0*		*694*
S	Specifications	Pro	*6.25*		*217*
		Secretary	*1.75*		*61*
B	Bids	Pro	*1.5*		*52*
		Parapro	*1.0*		*35*
A	Contract Administration	Pro	*8.0*		*277*
		Parapro	*16.0*		*555*

FIGURE 1-1 PROJECT TIME AND EXPENSE BUDGET.

the maximum number of hours that can be economically spent in each production phase. It can be debated that this form of budgeting is too simplified or that an average production-hour rate does not adequately differentiate between the professional and paraprofessional staff efforts. But record keeping and budgeting is not an exact science, and to maintain the necessary time and expense records in a manner that will more accurately produce the budget may be so time-consuming that for many offices it may be the choice between either keeping books or practicing architecture. A simple budget based on a simple but well-kept time and expense record can produce very reasonable results.

A carefully kept record of production hours on similar, completed projects is the most reliable measure of probable performance time on a new project. Once the total production-hour limit is established (the maximum number of hours allowed to produce the project at a profit), it becomes the boundary within which the number of available draftors, the number of office working days, and the completion date variables can be adjusted. However, the in-house drafting schedule is not independent; it must be coordinated with the concurrent efforts of the consultants in order to ensure a smooth flow of information and production.

Scheduling and budgeting is never *simple* arithmetic. Professionals and paraprofessionals vary in effective speed and ability; the progress of consultants is difficult to control; and necessary decisions from the owner or building officials may be delayed. Therefore, a degree of flexibility is necessary.

But there is a facet of time budgeting that *is* simple arithmetic. Once the time frame for working drawings is established, the progress within that time frame must be checked regularly, every few days, and the draftors should be kept aware of their performance. If 800 hours are budgeted for working drawings and the drawings are 50 percent completed with 500 hours consumed, a meeting of the minds is in order to determine what adjustments can be made to complete the drawings within the budgeted production-hour limit. It is axiomatic that *unless the working drawings phase shows a profit, the project will ultimately be produced at a loss.*

AN EFFICIENT DRAFTING STATION

An efficient drafting station is imperative to work production. In many office arrangements, the simple U-shaped area, as in Figure 1-2, can prove tremendously efficient. The station should be located close to catalogs, reference files, and supplies. Supplemental storage in the form of files below the tables and bookshelving above should be limited to the personal requirements of the

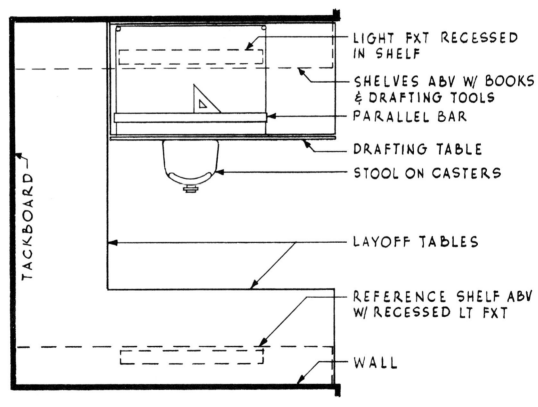

FIGURE 1-2 U-SHAPED DRAFTING STATION.

draftor. The available wall space should be lined with tackboard for pinning up plans, production schedules, and notes.

The proximity of coworkers is an important consideration in the assignment of drafting stations. In any office, trainees should be located close to their immediate supervisors. In large offices where each project requires a different team assignment, the team of draftors should be located close together with changes made in station occupancy as needed. Yet this territorial disturbance can be upsetting to the draftor, and a change of location may be resented. In such cases it is well to remember that the goal is efficiency and that the drafting station is simply a work station—not a sanctuary.

PROJECT RECORDS

The "Drawings and Specifications Outline" serves as the wellspring of information for the drafting force. It is here that the step-by-step decisions concerning materials and installation requirements are recorded and kept available for continual reference. This booklet should be organized by divisions and sections, coordinated with the CSI Format, and by the headings that are generally used by the individual office—with each heading followed by adequate space for the entries that will be written by hand. (Some headings will require more space than others.)

By the completion of the Design Development Phase, many decisions will have been made concerning materials and construction methods. These should already have been recorded in the "Outline" and now, at the beginning of the Construction Documents Phase, the project architect and the specifications writer should review the decisions and make additional entries (see Figure 1-3) as necessary to bring all information up to date. By this point, the project architect is well aware of the concept and the budget, knows the office policies, and has the experience to make many decisions the draftors will need to rely on. Each entry must be made precisely and methodically and should include:

The item or material and its accessories

Where and how it is to be used

The manufacturer's name and catalog number

The Sweet's Catalog File or other source where it may be found, including the index and the page number

The "Outline" should be kept as a separate booklet, well marked and readily available to the draftors and other project personnel throughout the drawing period. As each additional item is selected and each decision made on any installation method, the person

DIVISION 5 (cont'd)

MISCELLANEOUS METALS   Reference

Steel Railings:
  Balcony. Smooth welded joints, Steel tubing, paint   Dwg Dtl

Handrail brackets:
  Stairs S1 & S2. Ajax Ironworks AJ204, Dull Brz   Sweets 5.1/A1

Safety stair treads:
  Stair S3. Slip-Not Mfg SS1-04 aluminum   Mfr's Cat., Pg 6
  with Type 4 anchors

Access doors:
  Plumbing chase, Rm 107. AcDor MA117-2,   Sweets 8.12/AD
  16"W x 24"H, with key lock

FIGURE 1-3 SHEET FROM THE "DRAWINGS AND SPECIFICATIONS OUTLINE."

making the decision must make the appropriate brief entry in the "Outline" and make it promptly in order that the details of the decision not be lost. No decision should have to be made twice, and no decision should remain in someone's mind when it should be in the record—available to all. On completion of the drawings, this "Outline" will serve as a reference for the specifications writer, who will need to know what was used in the design and where to find the data related to it. It will also serve as a record for the project architect when making the checkout.

The "Project Booklet" (one or more books, such as large-ring loose-leaf notebooks) should be maintained throughout the project for the keeping of records in an orderly manner so that they may be available to the staff for continued reference. Many projects can be handled with a large notebook for the planning (Schematic Phase through Construction Documents phase) and another booklet for the Bid and Construction Phases. The "Planning Booklet," with which the draftor will be more concerned, may be organized by an index sheet, as in Figure 1-4, supplemented with tabbed dividers for each of the general categories.

At the inception of the project, the secretary can prepare the "Project Planning Booklet" by inserting the preprinted index sheet and typing a tabbed divider for each category. The organization of the booklet allows for quick reference during the planning and development of the drawings, and it facilitates the review during the checkout process. All calculations should appear neatly and on an established form of the office. The record (preferably typed) of all conferences and of all instructions or decisions received from the owner, building officials, contractors, consultants, supervisors, or others, should follow a standardized format and include:

Date

Names of those in attendance, or of those giving instructions or making decisions

A brief but complete statement of instructions, decisions, and observations

PLANNING BOOKLET INDEX

1. General Correspondence & Conferences
   a) General correspondence with Owner
   b) Correspondence with others
      (except as noted below)
   c) Personal conference summaries
   d) Telephone conference summaries
2. Formal Reports
   a) Reports to Owner
   b) Outline specifications
3. Program
   a) Owner's requirements
4. Research
   a) Notes of research trips
   b) Building type research
5. Design Data
   a) Design data
   b) Design calculations
   c) Space studies
   d) Measurements of existing building
6. Codes & Regulations
   a) Code requirements
   b) Ordinances and regulations
   c) Decisions and correspondence with
      regulatory officials
7. Site and Soil
   a) Surveys
   b) Legal descriptions
   c) Correspondence with consultant
   d) Soils engineering report
8. Structural
   a) Instructions to consultant
   b) Correspondence with consultant
   c) Structural calculations
9. Mechanical-Electrical
   a) Instructions to Mech-Elec consultants
   b) Correspondence with consultants
10. Special Consultants
    (Food Service, Acoustics, Landscaping, etc.)
    a) Instructions to consultants
    b) Correspondence with consultants
11. Cost Estimates
    a) Detailed estimates
    b) Statements of Probable Construction Cost
12. Photographs
13. Products
    a) Product brochures
    b) Correspondence with suppliers
14. Bids
    a) Prospective bidders list
    b) Bid information

FIGURE 1-4   INDEX SHEET FROM THE "PLANNING BOOKLET."

On completion of the project, all of these records should be placed in a durable binder in the permanent files. Many future occasions will require reference to these records.

FILING SYSTEMS

In the drafting area, three categories of reference filing are usually required and are listed as follows:

CSI System	*Project Numbers*	*Alphabetized*
Catalogs and brochures	Original tracings	Blank forms
	Microfilms	Research data (by building types)
Sample products	Project records	
Specification masters		

The sixteen divisions of the CSI system are easy to memorize, and the sections thereunder are logically related. The Sweet's Catalog File has the CSI numbering of divisions and sections on the binder edge of the volumes. Centrally locating the Sweet's File at eye level is expedient for many offices. In this position, it may serve as a reference index for the coordinated filing of other catalogs and samples when miscellaneous shelf catalogs are labeled on the binder edge and samples are tagged or labeled, each with the respective division number.

For identification of the tracings and other project records, a project number should be assigned from a consecutive master list as soon as the project is acquired. Since numbers are difficult to remember, a companion list, cross-indexed by alphabetized project names, will make for quick reference. Most offices store the original tracings in roll form, which requires considerable space and a measure of fire protection. Some offices convert the drawings to microfilms to conserve space, but although microfilms can be photoenlarged to reproduce the drawings, there are certain inaccuracies in the enlargements. Miniature negatives, which can be photoenlarged to the precise size of the original drawing, may gain widespread use in the future.

DRAFTING QUALITY

Although drafting can be improved by following detailed instructions and by observing good drawing techniques, the development of drafting excellence is largely the product of personal practice and self-improvement. A surprisingly short period of time is required to raise one's drafting to a highly presentable level. But there are no shortcuts; *the draftor must make the effort*.

Working drawings, as a communication medium, require a level of drafting quality that aids that communication; thus, the draftor must be able to draw and to letter neatly and accurately. Working drawings are not required to be a work of art—but this statement should not serve as an excuse for poor work quality.

The emphasis must be on *clear communication* with a minimum of lines and words. If one line or one word will suffice, two would be superfluous. The economy of effort will be appreciated by the employer and by the builder who must read the drawings.

Working drawings are not renderings; they are *diagrams* illustrating methods, materials, and equipment in the simplest, most clearly recognizable form. Only good judgment is necessary to determine what to *draw* and what to *letter*. A note, if it will make a complete communication, takes much less time to execute than a drawing. The arrangement of floor plans, sections, and schedules on the drawing sheet is important, but the fundamental characteristic of sheet composition should be *clarity,* not esthetics.

Generally the drawing is the important part of the visual communication; the lettered notes explain it, and the title identifies it. Therefore, the drawings should be illustrated clearly and powerfully; the note should be in proportion to the drawing and arranged to supplement it, not to compete with it; and the title should be bold, for a quick, positive identification. The drawing should be executed with confidence, without any feeble lines. Drawings are made to be reproduced, so an observation of the reproduced copy will reveal how the drafting looks in print. The draftor can be an effective *self-critic*.

Frequently the draftor will have labored long to produce a superb drawing only to be informed of a correction required by the structural engineer, or of a change made by the owner, which may necessitate much erasing and redrawing, resulting in a less-than-best final drawing. Rare is the fledgling draftor who can accept this mutilation of his or her masterpiece without developing a "hot collar." But the fundamental that must be accepted is that *the end product of the drawing effort is not the drawing itself but the production of the best possible building;* changes in the drawings will be inevitable in that process. The mature draftor produces quality drawings in spite of changes and adversities.

Not all drawings require the same quality of appearance. The builder will frequently require a supplemental clarification drawing, the cabinetmaker may need the detail of a special joint, or the client may want some quick "idea-arrangements" for the desks. These one-time or limited-use drawings are generally suited to a *shop-drawing* technique, accurately but very quickly drawn, and often noted in handwriting rather than lettering. The draftor must make certain of the purpose for which the drawing is intended, for few offices will appreciate the time it takes to produce an excellent delineation for a drawing of such limited use.

SPELLING

Communication is hindered by poor spelling. On completion, a drawing should be rechecked for proper spelling, and a dictionary should be consulted if there is doubt. A professional is *expected* to know how to spell at least those words of regular use.

DRAWINGS FOR THE BUILDER

Since the purpose of the drawings is to communicate to the builder proper instructions for producing the building, the draftor must be knowledgeable and sensitive to what drawings the builder needs to have, to what the builder needs to know. The drawings required for a multimillion-dollar hospital will be quite different from those required for a moderate-size private residence—the type and complexities of the construction will be markedly different, and the previous training and experience of the builder's staff, who will read and build from these drawings, is likely to be different for the two types of construction. The development of the working drawings should proceed only after a careful analysis of the needs of the specific project.

Information should be given to the builder wherever in the documents it is most logical and efficient to do so. For example, the wood panel covering on a partition might be noted on the floor plan: it might be noted in a detail, it would probably be designated in a room finish schedule, and it would undoubtedly be described in the specifications. Generally, the builder, the construction superintendent, and the trade mechanics study the floor plan and its accompanying room finish schedule rather carefully and frequently. But if a material or a construction method is not readily noticeable from the floor plan, they may not observe a related detail (important as it might be), and they may not fully relate tne material or method to its specification. Too often the drawings are hastily read and the specifications passed over. Space alone will limit the amount of information that can be indicated and noted on a floor plan, but it is axiomatic that the information on a floor plan is the most likely to be observed and will receive the most attention.

For any sizable project, the ability to quickly locate details and information contained in the drawings is important to the architectural staff during planning and construction, to the estimators, and to the construction personnel. During the course of a construction project, a single schedule may be referred to literally hundreds of times. Thus, a simple and efficient system of cross-referencing is mandatory (see Figure 2-6).

PROJECT DELIVERY SYSTEMS—CONVENTIONAL, FAST-TRACK, AND CONSTRUCTION MANAGEMENT

How the project will be built is a dominant factor in determining the methods and scheduling for the production of the drawings, and this question must be resolved at the very outset of the project. Most architects, engineers, and staff members are very familiar with the conventional services required for a construction project, including the production of drawings and specifications, the taking of bids and the awarding of contracts, and the administration of the project, including the making of field observations during the construction process. This type of service requires a very complete set of drawings and specifications so that all bidders can compete fairly and without confusion. Throughout this process, the architect/engineer maintains fundamental control of the design, exercises control over the selection of materials and equipment, and holds considerable power in judging the performance of the construction contract.

The time required to produce all the construction documents in advance of bidding and construction and the necessity of the architect/engineer's estimating the construction cost with no actual control over the costs of materials or contracting operations has given rise, in recent years, to other forms of project delivery systems such as Fast-Track (or Phased Construction) and construction management (CM).

Perhaps the following examination of these delivery systems will assist in introducing their fundamentals to the architects, engineers, and draftors who may not yet have experienced them. However, there are so many forms and combinations available in Fast-Track and CM projects that this or any other brief description must necessarily be oversimplified, and could tend to be misleading. Before anyone attempts to use such systems, he or she should exhaustively research other available data on the subject and discuss the technicalities with professionals who have previously been involved with them.

Fast-Track (a new name for a not-so-new system) has become increasingly popular for many construction projects. The principle is to get the construction under way, and to finish it, at the earliest possible dates. The probabilities of early completion and occupancy of the building, as well as the dollar savings this may represent, can be very attractive to the owner. To accomplish this end, the architectural services and the construction are telescoped into a coordinated schedule.

The principle of getting started early generally means that the construction will begin before a full set of construction documents can be made available. Materials that are scarce or that may require a long delivery schedule must be ordered well in advance, and to achieve this lead time, a form of *predetailed* drawings accompanied by brief specifications must be made available as soon as possible after the design concept has been formulated. This obviously requires a different approach to the entire design, drawing, and specification production process. Firm decisions on materials and methods must be made early in the design stages; therefore, later changes may be difficult. The drawings must be prepared in a format that will allow the dimensioned plans and details required for early bidding and the earliest stages of construction to be prepared first (such as those for site work, excavations, and foundations) and with a logical method for adding information as subsequent stages are more thoroughly planned. With the many adjustments that must be made to the drawings during the construction period of the Fast-Track process, a set of *as-built* drawings prepared by the architect/engineer at the completion of construction can be particularly important to the owner.

The possible limitations of the Fast-Track system include the following.

1. Using short-form drawings and specifications for the procurement of lead-time items may be too limiting for broad competitive bidding, or, conversely, the drawings and specifications may not be descriptive enough for good quality control.

2. By the time the drawings and specifications have progressed to the point where building inspectors, street and highway engineers, and other officials can give full approval to the intended materials and methods, the construction may have begun and proceeded to a point where nonapproval could cause extensive redesigning or even tearing out of the work-in-place. Similarly, any delay in issuing approvals could result in significant scheduling changes.

3. In the race to keep ahead of the builder, it is difficult to complete the drawings and to check them sufficiently to have confidence in their adequacy. For example, in the effort to enclose a building before winter, the construction schedule may require the building of the exterior fabric before a sufficient study of the details can be made to ensure their accuracy and their correlation with other parts of the building.

4. In the conventional method of developing working drawings, the design professional may improve the design and details as better ideas occur, until the time the project is ready for bids. In the Fast-Track situation, where the construction has already begun, many of these changes, which are implemented by change orders, cannot be introduced without causing chaos in the construction program. In other words, it may be more difficult to improve the product.

An architect-contractor team, by rephasing and properly modifying its conventional services, can perform Fast-Track, but the success of integrating and expediting the design and construction schedules is largely dependent on aggressive project management, which requires an expertise many conventional firms may lack. The ability to efficiently administer Fast-Track and the breaking of the bidding into smaller-than-conventional packages to increase the competition have been two key factors contributing to the increased use of construction management.

Although the construction management (CM) system should not be applied to every kind of project, it is particularly appropriate for complex long-term projects where time and continuity of control are of the essence. The system is a managerial service, over and above normal architectural and engineering services related to the construction program. It integrates the predesign, design, and construction phases of the building project under a single administrative body (the construction management) that contributes to the control of time and cost in the construction. The system involves the employment of an independent professional construction manager (who in some cases may be the general contractor or even the architect). Theoretically, the architect/engineer, the construction manager, and the owner are a team working for the benefit of the project, and the success of the venture is highly dependent on the team members being able to work well together. As team coordinator, the construction manager administers the designs, schedules, and budgets that express quality, time, and cost in a flexible yet logical format that all team members can understand and work with. The construction manager is fundamentally responsible for team communications, for keeping and distributing to the others the minutes of all meetings, for updating the schedules, and for advising the others of costs and budgets.

Working cooperatively from the inception of the project, the construction manager and the architect/engineer develop a building concept in accordance with the owner's program and budget. During the preplanning phase the construction manager can be particularly instrumental in defining and analyzing the scope of the project and in giving professional advice to the owner and to the architect/engineer on design considerations that will affect the initial cost, long term values, and construction procedures.

Throughout the early design processes the construction management will request the architect/engineer to make alternative schemes for materials and systems which will be tested by the construction manager against the requirements and the budget of the project. By this method, intelligent trade-offs and alterations can be made before materials and systems have become fixed. In this process, the construction manager will apply the principles of value engineering (meeting the owner's values at the least possible cost) and energy conservation in terms of life-cycle costing—in each case testing quality against time and budget by selecting from the various alternatives and by recycling the process as necessary until compatibility emerges. For example, the construction manager may request the architect to design several different plan arrangements or structural systems in order to evaluate the probable costs and construction time schedules required by each scheme. Some architect/engineers will resent these intrusions on their professional creativity, but if the owner, the construction manager, and the architect/engineer can cooperatively work under the pressure of a production schedule, decisions can usually be made quickly and logically—and this can mean a significant savings in time and money for the architect/engineer's office as well as a benefit to the owner. A further resentment on the part of the architect/engineers may develop if decisions are consistently influenced by initial cost and made at the expense of quality and esthetics.

Responsible and timely estimating is one of the construction management's most impressive tools. The ability to establish a probable cost for the various concepts and alternatives in the early periods of the design program can avoid many potential problems. As the cooperative thought and decision-making processes continue through the Design Development Phase, the architect/engineer will produce an almost completely dimensioned series of floor plans and elevations, together with supplemental detail sheets; diagrammatic layouts of the structural, mechanical, and electrical systems; and a booklet outlining the room finishes and equipment, catalog cuts of plumbing and electrical fixtures, manufacturers' data sheets on heating and air conditioning equipment, and other information necessary to generally establish the construction. At this point, the drawings are not very complete but are sufficient for the general concept of the project. This is the earliest point at which a guaranteed maximum price can be established and the construction started, but usually this pricing and starting point should be delayed until a considerably larger number of working drawings have been completed. Obviously, the more complete the documents, the less of a contingency factor the construction management will need to include in the price.

During the construction period the architect/engineer must guard the integrity of the design by approving shop drawings, evaluating change order proposals, and making field observations; but mechanics of bidding, contracting, management, and bookkeeping are largely the duties of the construction manager. The construction manager should have primary inspection responsibility for the subcontracts and crafts, and therefore the involvement of the architect/engineer in field work may (in certain projects) be substantially reduced. Changes and change orders will be inevitable, and the procedures for executing these change documents must be clearly defined and well understood by all parties. Depending on the circumstances, a change order may be initiated by the construction manager, by the architect/engineer, or by the owner, but generally the architect/engineer will be called on to revise the details and to otherwise document the change order to be signed by the owner. The architect/engineer's involvement is essential in order to maintain coordination of the drawings and specifications and to produce the as-built drawings at the conclusion of the project (if as-builts are required).

Network planning through the Critical Path Method (CPM) of scheduling can be an important tool in establishing and monitoring the construction program. Although this system is well known in the construction industry, it is also applicable to the architect/engineer's office in planning and monitoring its activities throughout large and complex design projects. In Fast-Track and CM systems a periodically updated CPM chart will graphically illustrate to the owner and to the design-construction team the phasing and time control essentials of the project.

Fast-Track is frequently used in the CM system, and as a result all the advantages and disadvantages previously expressed for Fast-Track become applicable to construction management. The savings in time, if they materialize, are usually attributable to the use of Fast-Track, coupled with aggressive and competent management techniques.

Under a pure CM contract, the construction manager is retained as a professional to provide estimating and scheduling services during the design phase of the project and to provide coordination among the various speciality contractors performing the actual construction work under separate contracts with the owner. The construction manager may also be required to supervise the construction. Under this contract the construction management's own forces are not permitted to perform any of the construction activities, and the construction management does not provide a guaranteed maximum price or a guaranteed time of completion.

Under a modified CM contract, the construction manager is again required to provide estimating and scheduling services during the design period and to construct the project and perform all the coordination and supervision of the subcontractors. Generally the construction management's own forces may be permitted to perform portions of the work, and the construction management may be required to provide a guaranteed maximum price and a guaranteed time of completion. The subcontracts are held by the construction manager, who is fully responsible for the performance of the subs, much as a general contractor would be.

Under still another modification of the CM contract, a general contractor assumes primary involvement, with the construction manager performing as a part of the contractor's team. In this system the performance of the construction manager during the design processes is similar to that under the above options (indeed, an independent professional construction manager may be employed during these phases), but during the construction process the coordination of the subcontracting and in-house forces may be more expeditious if the construction manager is a part of the contractor's team.

It might be said that an architect/engineer–contractor team approach would automatically provide construction management to the owner. This could be highly effective to the right owner with the right combination of architect/engineer and contractor. However, this approach should not be confused with that of the construction manager providing a professional service to the owner. Under a general contract, the contractor is required to construct the building and provide a guaranteed maximum price and a guaranteed date of completion. In most cases this contractor is not employed until the contract documents have been completed.

The inevitable concern about final costs on the part of the owner and the architect/engineer is alleviated when the construction manager establishes the guaranteed maximum price at an early stage. Thereafter, the architect/engineer can proceed expeditiously through the contract documents with the relative assurance that the project cost will be within the budget and that the detailing will be simplified where materials and equipment have already been selected. Although the drafting system required for Fast-Track or construction management is basically the same as for a conventional system of architectural drawings, every Fast-Track or CM project will be organized differently, and some of the drawing procedures will need to be modified, which may include:

1. Preparing schematic and design development drawings by predetailing, similar to Figure 6-1.

2. Establishing on the plan drawings a grid system, or identification zone system, or both, in order that later developed plans and details may be related to and keyed to earlier drawings, thereby avoiding any confusions as to where later drawings apply.

3. Developing the drawings with the requirements for further additions and changes in mind. Using reproducible sepias and the cut-and-paste photo process may aid in making changes, and preparing the original drawings on a very durable sheet, such as polyester-base drafting film, will prove beneficial when repeated changes are made.

4. Organizing drawings and specifications in a manner to facilitate "contract packaging" that will allow bidding in construction sequences and will clearly define the "interfacing" between contracts.

To further illustrate the differences, Table 1-1 compares the construction management and conventional delivery systems as they might be applied to a hypothetical project. In this illustration the CM method assumes the participation of an architect/engineer and a construction management–general contractor team. Similarly, the construction management could involve an independent professional service, and there are many other possible team combinations, many other options for specific involvement and responsibilities between team members, and other available possibilities in sequencing and phasing for this and other projects.

TABLE 1-1   Comparison between Construction Management and Conventional Delivery Systems

| Phase | Responsibility by Method* | | | | | |
| | CM | | | Conventional | | |
	Owner	A/E	CM	Owner	A/E	Contr.
Preplanning or Conceptual						
Owner's program (consultant)	P	O	O	P	O	O
Owner's budget	P	O	O	P	O	O
Analyze program vs. budget	P	P	P			
Evaluate site and utilities	O	P	P			
Coordinate with govt. agencies	O	P	M			
Space relationships studies	O	P	O			
Conceptual estimate	O	O	P			
Evaluate budget vs. estimate	P	P	P			
Feasibility and financing	P	O	M	P	O	O
Preliminary master schedule	M	M	P			
Presentation/report	O	P	P			
Owner's review and approval	P					
Schematic Design						
Design schedule	O	P	P	O	P	O
Site information				P	M	O
Evaluate site and utilities				O	P	O
Review codes and zoning				O	P	O
Research building type	O	P	O	O	P	O
Interview project users	O	P	O	O	P	O
Involve systems consultants	O	P	O	O	P	O
Space/flow relationship studies	O	P	O	O	P	O
Embryonic concept	O	P	M	O	P	O
Study models and sketches	O	P	O	O	P	O

*Responsibility: P = prime; M = minor; O = none.

Phase	Responsibility by Method					
	CM			Conventional		
	Owner	A/E	CM	Owner	A/E	Contr.
Owner's program (consultant)	P	O	O	P	O	O
Owner's budget	P	O	O	P	O	O
Analyze program vs. budget	P	P	P			
Evaluate design data	O	P	M	O	P	O
Evaluate unit costs	O	P	P	O	P	O
Schematic drawings	O	P	O	O	P	O
Predetailing	O	P	M			
Outline specifications	M	P	M			
Cost estimate	O	O	P	O	P	O
Recommend materials and systems	O	P	P	O	P	O
Adjust program/budget/estimate	P	P	P	P	P	O
Retain special consultants	M	P	M	P	P	O
Environmental study	O	P	O	O	P	O
Economic energy study	O	P	P	O	P	O
Value engineering	O	P	P	O	P	O
Prepare/analyze alternate schemes	O	P	P	O	P	O
Reporting and accounting procedures	M	M	P			
Identify long-lead purchase items	O	M	P			
Prepare bid package format	O	P	P			
Phased construction schedule	O	M	P			
Review govt., utility, and insurance requirements	M	P	M	M	P	O
Update estimate/schedule/budget	P	P	P	P	P	O
Presentation/report	O	P	P	O	P	O
Owner's review and approval	P			P		

TABLE 1-1   Comparison between Construction Management and Conventional Delivery Systems (*Continued*)

Phase	Responsibility by Method*					
	CM			Conventional		
	Owner	A/E	CM	Owner	A/E	Contr.
Design Development						
Refine program per budget/estimate	P	P	P	P	P	O
Update design schedule	O	P	P	O	P	O
Research materials/methods				O	P	O
Reevaluate components, systems, and system alternates	O	P	P	O	P	O
Value engineering analysis	O	M	P	O	P	O
Final select components and systems	P	P	P	P	P	O
Consultants develop basic systems	O	P	O	O	P	O
Design development drawings	O	P	O	O	P	O
Model or rendering	O	P	O	O	P	O
Outline specifications by finishes/ equipment				M	P	O
Establish "general conditions"	M	M	P			
Refine outline specifications	O	P	M			
Preliminary construction estimate	O	O	P			
Preliminary construction schedule	O	O	P			
Coordinate with agencies and utilities	O	P	M			
Evaluate labor and trade market	O	O	P			
Trade contractor bid lists	M	O	P			
Update master schedule	O	O	P			
Analyze program/budget/estimate	P	P	P	P	P	O
Refine project budget	P	M	P	P	M	O

	Responsibility by Method					
	CM			Conventional		
Phase	*Owner*	*A/E*	*CM*	*Owner*	*A/E*	*Contr.*
Long-lead purchase and phased construction documents	O	P	M			
Assurance of project financing	P	O	O	P	O	O
Presentation/report	O	P	P	O	P	O
Owner's review and approval	P			P		
Contract Documents						
Coordinate/schedule drawing/spec. production	O	P	M	O	P	O
Revise drawings to accurate scale and dimension				O	P	O
Obtain partial building permit	M	O	P			
Implement phased construction	M	M	P			
Bid/purchase long-lead items	M	M	P			
Supply consultants with accurate drawings	O	P	O	O	P	O
Develop drawing control diagrams	O	P	O	O	P	O
Receive diagrams from consultants	O	P	O	O	P	O
Develop working drawings	O	P	O	O	P	O
Develop specifications				O	P	O
Coordinate drawings with specifications	O	P	O	O	P	O
Coordinate with consultants	O	P	O	O	P	O
Close out and check out drawings and specs	O	P	O	O	P	O
Review drawings and specifications	P	M	P	P	M	O
Finalize budget/estimates	P	M	P	P	P	O

TABLE 1-1   Comparison between Construction Management and Conventional Delivery Systems (*Continued*)

| | Responsibility by Method | | | | | |
| | CM | | | Conventional | | |
Phase	Owner	A/E	CM	Owner	A/E	Contr.
Finalize owner occupancy schedule	P	O	P	P	M	O
Cash flow schedule	M	O	P			
Finalize trade contractor bid lists	M	M	P			
Final govt. agency review/approval	M	P	M	O	P	O
Final insurance review	P	M	M	P	M	O
Update construction schedule	O	O	P			
Procure final building permit	M	O	P			
Bid market analysis	O	O	P			
Contract document report	O	P	P	O	P	O
Owner's review and approval	P			P		
Bidding and Award						
Solicit trade contractor bids	M	O	P			
Solicit contract bids				M	P	O
Conduct prebid conference	O	O	P	O	P	O
Receive and tabulate bids	M	M	P	M	P	O
Update construction and master schedule	O	O	P			
Owner's review and approval	P			P		
Issue contract or notice to proceed	P	O	O	P	O	O
Detailed construction schedule	O	O	P	O	O	P
Preaward conference	M	M	P			
Award trade contracts	M	O	P	O	O	P
Construction						
Mobilize for construction	O	O	P	O	O	P
Verify insurance requirements	P	O	P	P	M	P

	Responsibility by Method					
	CM			Conventional		
Phase	Owner	A/E	CM	Owner	A/E	Contr.
Approve progress payments	P	O	P	O	P	O
Review/approve shop drawings and samples	O	P	P	O	P	P
Project cost control	O	O	P			
Evaluate/update progress schedule	O	O	P	O	M	P
Change orders	P	M	P	P	P	P
Inspect and monitor subcontract work	O	O	P	O	O	P
Observe design conformance	O	P	M	O	P	O
Interpret plans & specifications	O	P	M	O	P	M
Administer safety/security programs	O	O	P	O	O	P
Coordinate owner occupancy schedule	P	O	P	P	M	P
Certify substantial completion	M	P	P	M	P	O
Final inspection	M	P	P	P	P	M
Prepare punch list	O	M	P	O	M	P
Start-up & recommend maintenance	M	M	P	M	M	P
As-built drawings	O	P	P			
Assemble manuals & warranties	O	O	P	O	M	P
Final accounting	M	O	M	O	P	O
Owner's review & approval	P	O	O	P	O	O
Post Construction						
Perform guarantee requirements	O	O	P			
Provide continuing consultation	O	O	P			

2

DRAWING SHEETS AND SHEET ORGANIZATION

2 | DRAWING SHEETS AND SHEET ORGANIZATION

DRAWING PAPERS

The selection of the drawing paper will vary according to individual preference. Where the emphasis is on the use of pencil rather than ink, the need will be for a very durable paper that will precisely record the one-stroke penciled and printed lines yet will accept ink equally well. For many, Clearprint 1000PH will meet these requirements for regular use, while Clearprint 1020 can be used when heavier-weight durability is desired. The requirement for greater transparency when tracing over other drawings and for greater stability and durability (including erasability) may favor the use of drafting films instead of paper. Although matte finish films will accept either pencil or ink, the hardness of the film requires greater care and greater pressure to produce a quality pencil drawing. Therefore, when a more durable tracing is required, economy may favor making the original drawing in pencil on a fine grade paper, then photocopying it on drafting film (see Chapter 7).

SHEET SIZES

The size of the drawing sheet needs careful consideration. In terms of drawing, the sheet must be large enough to accommodate the various plans, schedules, and details of the project, but it must not be so large as to require the draftor to frequently reach across it to draw in the uppermost areas (neither the use of a vertical-tilt board nor the procedure of rolling the lower edge of the sheet into a containing tube is a thoroughly satisfactory substitute for a drawing sheet of the proper size). In terms of filing, the size should be convenient size for tabletop reference and vertical, hanging-rack storage during the construction period, and should fold to a size that allows them to be filed in letter-size drawers with the other project records and mailed with correspondence. Filing is made difficult by using different sizes of sheets for different projects, even if they are standard sizes. Roll files, flat files, and plan racks of different sizes will be necessary to accommodate the sheets, or larger files (thereby used inefficiently) will be required.

For all of these reasons, the popular 36 × 24″ and the supplementary 8½ × 11″ drawing sheets are recommended as standard sizes, with a larger-size sheet used only for very special projects. Normal-size projects with floor plans drawn at the scale of ⅛″ = 1'-0″ and residences drawn at ¼″ = 1'-0″ will usually fit conveniently on this sheet size. Even very large projects, drawn at an appropriate scale and with careful layout, can fit on this sheet size. Especially large or extended floor plans can have areas, or *zones,* of the plan drawn on separate sheets, all coordinated by a miniature *zone plan.* Even projects that might fit a smaller size sheet should be drawn instead on the 36 × 24″ sheet for the convenience of size uniformity in handling, filing, and mailing. The 8½ × 11″ sheet should be reserved for drawing details, schedules, etc., that may be bound with the specifications or bound in other booklet form.

By using a uniform and standard sheet size, precut drawing sheets are available as well as precut print paper, which again makes for convenience and economy. By adopting a uniform size, borders and title blocks can be printed on the drawing sheets in quantity.

BORDERS AND TITLE BLOCKS

The design of the border and especially of the title block should be individual to each office, for it can, and should, be a graphic of identification. Although some will prefer no borders, the border serves a visual function, similar to that of a picture frame, and it minimizes the appearance of torn and frayed edges that will occur with most drawings during the production process.

A workable border arrangement, indicated in Figure 2-1, allows a wider binding margin on the left. The title block might appear along

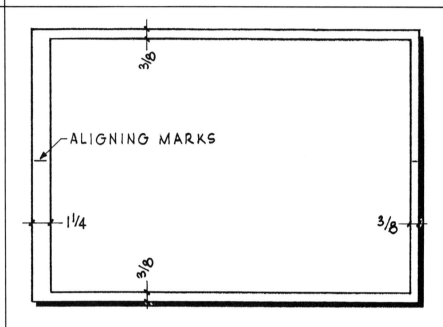

FIGURE 2-1 BORDERING THE DRAWING SHEET.

the bottom, at the lower right corner or along the right side; in any event, it would appear inside the border margins indicated. The completely filled-in title block should include at least this information:

Firm name and address

Sheet number

Project name and address

Project number

Release date

The seals of the appropriate architect and/or engineer must appear on the drawings. In addition, the title block may include identification of the draftor and checker and space for revision notations.

If the sheet is not preprinted, hand bordering should be done in very bold pencil or preferably in ink. Immediately after bordering any sheet, a short, sharp *aligning mark* (Figure 2-1) should be drawn along the straightedge in the left and right margins to ensure continued realignment accuracy. These marks should be included in the preprinting of bordered and titled sheets.

ORGANIZATION OF THE SHEETS

Projects vary so widely that no fixed rule can apply to the sequence of the finished sheets. Major projects may require a title sheet devoid of drawings and a rather clear separation (by sheets or even by divisions, following the CSI indexing) of plans, schedules, and details. A smaller project may place more information or, often, drawings on the cover sheet, and the separation of plans, schedules, and details may be less defined for economy of sheet space. Residential drawings are usually less structured in their organization, and frequently include electrical and mechanical symbols with the floor plans. In general, floor plans should follow one another progressively (lowest to highest floor) and appear early in the drawing set because of their frequency of use. The site plan may be placed first or last depending on its importance, and details should be grouped according to their relationship to each other, with minor details appearing last in the architectural series. Structural, mechanical, and electrical drawings will be produced concurrently with the architectural drawings, and therefore can best be organized within their individual groupings, then assembled as the last drawings. Accordingly, an arrangement for each of the two basic project types is suggested in Table 2-1. The numbers in the table indicate only the sequence of the drawings, not the separation of sheets or the number of sheets required for each listing.

As soon as the mock-up sheets (Figure 2-3) are roughed out, the sheet numbers should be assigned and the corresponding numbers subsequently penciled on the tracings-in-work, with these penciled numbers remaining until all extra sheets have been

TABLE 2-1   Sequence Arrangement of Drawings, by Project Types

All Projects (except Residential)	Residential Project
1. Project title, address, and owner; names of officials, drawing index; reference system; other general references.	1. Exterior elevations, project title, owner, and address; reference system.
2. Site plan; soil-boring log, site details; planting diagram.	2. Floor plans; special notes; room finish schedule.
3. Floor plans; partition indications; special notes; room finish schedules.	3. Basement or foundation plan; foundation details.
4. Reflected ceiling plans.	4. Building sections; wall sections; roof/wall intersections.
5. Roof plan, roof details.	5. Window details; door details.
6. Exterior elevations.	6. Stair details.
7. Building sections; wall sections; roof/wall intersections.	7. Interior elevations; interior details.
8. Window details.	8. Millwork and cabinet details.
9. Door schedules; door and frame details.	9. Miscellaneous details.
10. Elevator and stair details.	10. Site plan, site details.
11. Interior elevations; interior details.	11. Floor and roof-framing plan; framing diagrams.
12. General millwork and cabinet details.	12. Heating/cooling plan and details.
13. Miscellaneous details.	13. Other mechanical and electrical details.
14. Structural drawings; foundation plan, floor and roof-framing plans; details.	*Note:* plumbing and electrical fixtures, and electrical switching are to be indicated on floor plans.
15. Plumbing plans and details.	
16. Heating/cooling plans and details.	
17. Electrical plans and details.	
18. Food service plans and details.	
19. Special contract drawings.	

added. Then the sheet numbers should be boldly inked using this numbering system:

1,	2,	3, etc.	Architectural
S1,	S2,	S3, etc.	Structural
M1,	M2,	M3, etc.	Mechanical
E1,	E2,	E3, etc.	Electrical
FS1,	FS2,	FS3, etc.	Food service

Frequently the same site plan sheet will be used to illustrate both the mechanical and the electrical. In that case, the sheet should be numbered ME1 and the subsequent sheets M2, M3, etc., and E2, E3, etc.

Furnishings and special equipment may be handled by separate contracts, but whether the drawings are included with or are separate from the building construction documents, they can be coordinated by being numbered F1, F2, F3, etc., for furnishings and EQ1, EQ2, EQ3, etc., for equipment.

For all but the briefest set of drawings, a drawings index, similar to that in Figure 2-2, will be necessary. The listing should be divided by appropriate headings and should describe the principal features of each sheet. Ink stylography is appropriate for major projects, while pencil lettering may be acceptable for minor projects.

The titling on the cover sheet and the completion of the title blocks on the individual sheets is best done by one draftor for uniformity of appearance. Special attention should be given to the cover sheet in regard to composition and content. Depending on the project, stylographic ink, heat-resistant transfer (press-on) letters, or even pencil lettering may be appropriate. When special projects require a title block at variance with the office standard, film transfer sheets of the special title block can be made photographically (see Chapter 7), or even having the sheets printed with the border and special title block may be expedient. The project identification will be repeated so often in the title block, specifica-

A DRAWINGS INDEX

ARCHITECTURAL

    1 TITLE SHEET, REFERENCE SYSTEM
    2 SITE PLAN, SOIL BORINGS, PLANTINGS
    3 1st FLOOR PLAN, FINISH SCHEDULE
       ETC., ETC.

STRUCTURAL

    S1 FOUNDATION PLAN
    S2 PEDESTAL, GRADE BEAMS
       ETC., ETC.

MECHANICAL

    ME1 SITE PLAN, MECH & ELEC
    M2 1st FLOOR PLAN
    M3 2nd FLOOR PLAN
       ETC., ETC.

ELECTRICAL

    E2 1st FLOOR PLAN, LIGHTING
    E3 1st FLOOR PLAN, POWER
       ETC., ETC.

FIGURE 2-2 DRAWINGS INDEX.

tions, and project correspondence that it deserves to be condensed; for example, "The Center for Diagnostic and Therapeutic Radiology, Roosevelt and Highland Streets, Old Town, Kansas," might be reworded as "Radiology Center 1010 Highland, Old Town, KS."

ORGANIZATION ON THE SHEETS

In the Design Development Phase the floor plans, basic building sections, and some of the principal details are established to the extent that at the inception of the working drawings phase the project captain can reasonably anticipate the number and size of drawings required for the project. The captain should carefully prepare a mock-up outline of each sheet, as in Figure 2-3, illustrating in rough, outlined pencil form the plans, schedules, and detail spaces. Usually, additional development will be necessary before every necessary detail can be identified, but the outlining of the mock-up sheets should not be delayed; the unknown details can be added to the mock-ups as they develop. Some unplanned-for miscellaneous details will usually be relegated to the last sheet of the drawings, but experience and forethought in the preparation of the mock-ups can avoid gross disorganization.

The mock-up layouts should be prepared on standard-size sheets of opaque white paper using a freehand, soft-pencil technique to outline the plans, schedules, and details at reasonably accurate scale in order to adequately adjudge the space requirements. The arrangement should show a logical relationship among the details in an easy-to-read manner. Arranging the drawings in a compact or condensed manner is a virtue, for it reduces the number of sheets needed and thus the number of reproduced sheets. (The reproduction costs can be considerable for any project.)

A consistent orientation for the site plan, building plans, and related details will help avoid confusion. Generally the floor plan is placed with its front, or entrance, facing the lower edge of the sheet, and the site plan should be drawn correspondingly. Occasionally the ratio of length to width of the site, or of the floor plan, can require different orientations in order to fit the respective plans to the drawing sheets. In any case, a north arrow should accompany the site plan and each foundation and each floor plan. Details do not require north arrows unless the orientation is inconsistent with the related plan.

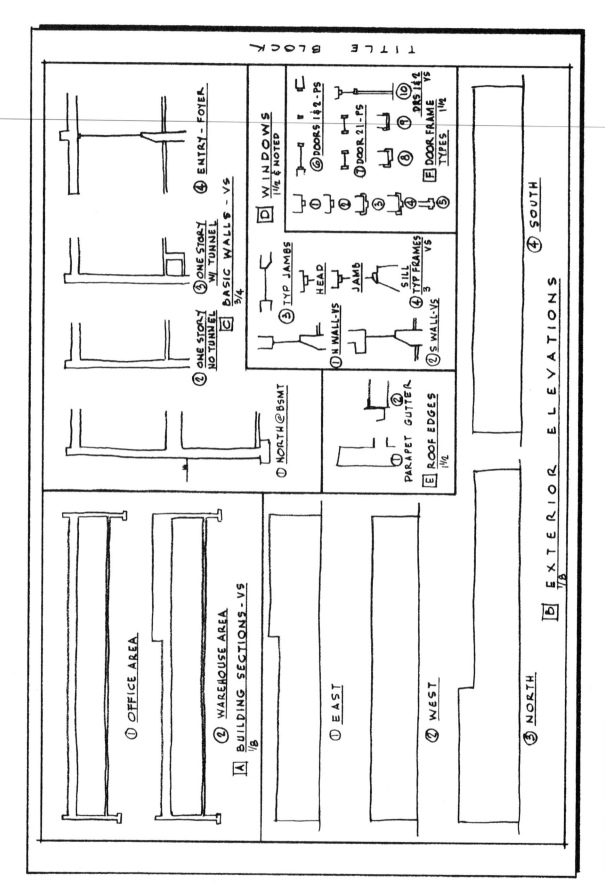

FIGURE 2-3A MOCK-UP SHEET.

40

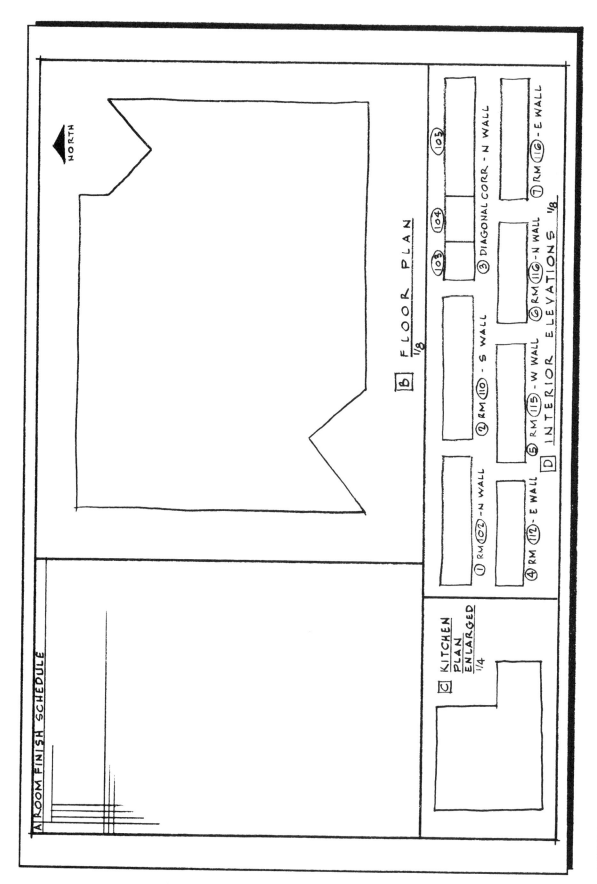

FIGURE 2-3B   MOCK-UP SHEET.

41

For convenience, the floor plans, which are the most used of all the drawings, should be placed at the right side of the sheet. The corresponding room finish schedule (as in Figure 2-3b) should appear on the same sheet as the floor plan as a further convenience for relating schedule to plan.

Each individual detail and each related series of details should be within a separate border on the sheet and appropriately identified by an individual or a group title, respectively. The letters and numbers of the identification system and the drawing scale should be added at this early stage.

Although the emphasis is on clarity and economy of sheet utilization, a degree of aesthetic arrangement can be planned into the drawing organization on any sheet. Figure 2-3 illustrates two examples of sheet layout where the groupings are compact, orderly, and attractive.

IDENTIFICATION SYSTEM

Plans, elevations, details, and schedules must be properly identified, as indicated in Figure 2-4, with a title preceded by a *boxed* letter. The *subdetails* (a related group of details under a single major title) must be similarly identified, but with an *encircled* number rather than with the boxed letter. The boxed-letter and encircled-number identifications should be assigned in sequence as the layouts of the mock-up sheets are prepared and should be continued on the drawings sheets as each plan, detail, etc., is drawn. Generally the organization will be from *left to right* and from *upper to lower* on the sheet. The sequence of identification letters begins anew on each sheet and the sequence of identification numbers anew within each detail group. The arrangement of details and the later addition of details may occasionally place the letters of identification out of sequence on the sheet, but this will be of little concern.

The identification letters, numbers, and titles may be penciled or inked. For major projects, stylographic inking of the letters, numbers, and titles (penciling the box and circle) may be preferred. On normal projects pencil will be convenient for all but the identification letter, which may be in stylographic ink for bolder identification. All titles and subtitles should be underlined for prominence. When ink is to be used, the identification should be lightly penciled at the time the drawing is made, allowing all inking to be done later at one time.

The sizes of lettering, boxes, and circles shown in Figure 2-4 are proper for many circumstances, but must be varied as necessary for space requirements, and must be *in scale* with the drawings. A consistent size should be used wherever practical.

The title of the plan, schedule, or detail must clearly identify the

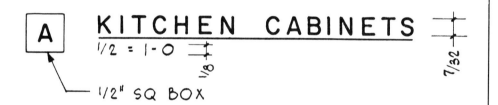

(a) Titles for plans, elevations, schedules and details

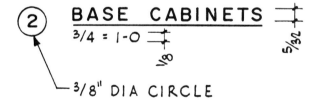

(b) Titles for subdetails

FIGURE 2-4   IDENTIFICATION OF THE DRAWING ELEMENTS.

drawing. Typical details apply at various locations, but wherever possible the titles should be more specific. Examples:

Ambiguous	*Clearly Identified*
Storage Shelving	Shelving, Rm 102
Door Frame	Jamb, Door 12
Front Stoop Sec	North Stoop—VS

Overuse of the word "detail" should be avoided. Essentially, all drawing enlargements are details. Thus, a detailed drawing of a

B SCALE OF DRAWINGS

THESE DRAWINGS MAY BE REPRODUCED
AT EITHER 24" x 36" OR 12" x 18" SHEET SIZES.
THEREFORE, BELOW EACH TITLE THE SCALE
IS STATED THUS :

HOWEVER, DWGS SHOULD ONLY BE SCALED
FOR GENERAL REFERENCE; USE DIMENSIONS
FOR ACTUAL ESTIMATING & CONSTRUCTION

FIGURE 2-5 SCALE OF DRAWINGS NOTATION FOR DRAWINGS REPRODUCED AT EITHER FULL-SIZE OR AT 50 PERCENT REDUCTION.

storage cabinet will be obviously recognized as a detail and does not need to be labeled "storage cabinet detail."

The title must indicate how the drawing reads: vertical section (VS), plan section (PS), elevation (EL), etc. These position indications must be appended to every title unless the title otherwise indicates the position of the drawing; for example, "floor plan," "door jamb," and "exterior elevations" are self-explanatory.

The scale of the drawing should accompany each drawing title. When a group of related drawings, such as exterior elevations, appear on a sheet at the same scale, but individually titled, the drawing scale may be handled by a general note, such as "scale elevations: $\frac{1}{8}$ = 1-0." Otherwise, the scale accompanying each title, such as "$\frac{3}{4}$ = 1-0," can be well understood without prefixing the word "scale." Where a series of subdetails are drawn at the same scale, one scale indication under the main detail title is sufficient. When most, but not all, subdetails are at the same scale, the scale indication may appear as "$\frac{3}{4}$ = 1-0, except noted."

Frequently drawings will be reproduced at both full and half sizes. In such cases, it may be more convenient for the builder to have each element of the drawing identified by both scales, as in Figure 2-5, rather than by a graphic scale. The explanation for the "reduced scale system" (Figure 2-5), then, should appear early in the drawings. However, if the reproduction is likely to be reduced in any other proportion, the graphic scale will be essential.

REFERENCE SYSTEM

The reference system, shown in Figure 2-6, must be prominently displayed on the drawings, preferably on the cover sheet. The reference system is used so repeatedly in preparing the working drawings and in reading the drawings during the later bidding and construction period that it should be simplified and standardized. Although Figure 2-6 uses architectural sheet numbers in the referencing system, the basic system likewise applies to structural, mechanical, electrical, and other special contract drawings; for example, typical referencing numbers might be S1A4, M3C12, or E2B3, respectively.

Several indications and options of the reference system are shown in the floor plan of Figure 2-7. The section-cutting planes and other references to details must be indicated on plans, elevations, and details as the circumstances require. When a detail applies to several locations or to a continuous element (for example, a typical eave section may apply to most or all of the roof perimeter), the cutting plane needs to be indicated only at a few obvious locations. The system is especially suited to directing attention to the appropriate details even when space is limited; for example, the note "CBT ABV" accompanied by the reference "11F2" (enclosed in a rectangle) clearly identifies that the wall

⬛A⬛ REFERENCE SYSTEM

SECTION IS DETAIL ⬛A⬛ ON SHEET 6

⬛6A3⬛ REFER TO SHEET 6, DETAIL ⬛A⬛ , SUBDETAIL ③

⬛7B⬛ ENLARGED DETAIL OF ENCIRCLED ELEMENT IS DETAIL ⬛B⬛ ON SHEET 7

REFER TO SPECIFICATIONS APPENDIXES AP1 AND AP2 FOR ABBREVIATIONS AND SYMBOLS

FIGURE 2-6   REFERENCE SYSTEM.

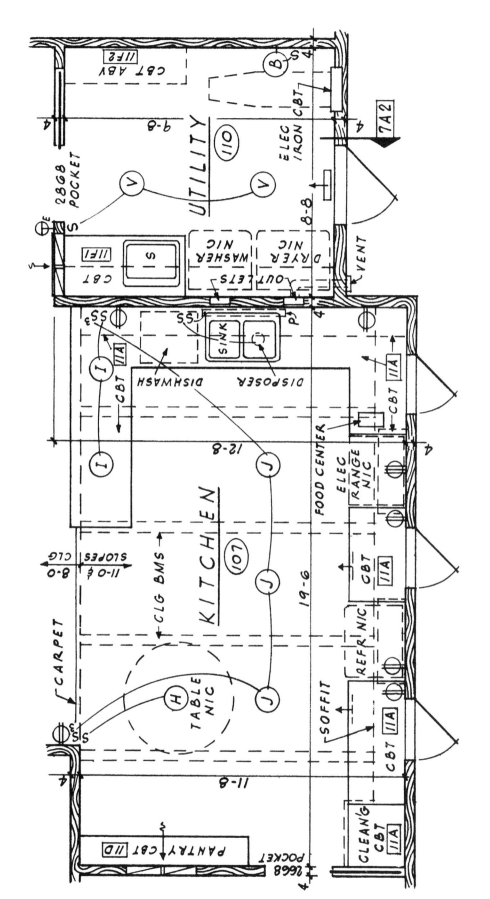

FIGURE 2-7 A COMPLEX FLOOR PLAN, CAREFULLY ORGANIZED AND REFERENCED.

cabinet above will be shown in greater detail on Drawing Sheet 11, Detail F, Subdetail 2.

As the drawings reach the closeout stage with all details substantially in place, a very thorough and systematic review must be made to determine that each and every drawing element is cross-referenced. Bidding and building the project will be made much easier through a coordinated use of the reference system.

3

DEVELOPING THE DRAWING AND LETTERING TECHNIQUE

3 | DEVELOPING THE DRAWING AND LETTERING TECHNIQUE

TOOLS OF THE TRADE

To produce quality drafting and to produce it efficiently, an assortment of good instruments and accessories is needed. The following is a list of the types and sizes of working tools most architectural draftors will find beneficial. In some instances, trade names are given to indicate a type of tool; other equivalent tools may be available.

12″ 30°-60° clear plastic triangle

12″ 45°-90° clear plastic triangle

10″ adjustable clear plastic triangle

12″ flat, tapered-edge, architectural scale, ⅛″ through 3″

12″ flat, tapered-edge, architectural scale, ¹⁄₁₆″

12″ flat, or triangular, engineer's scale

Brick coursing scale

Fugle, Leadlok, mechanical pencil (for drawing)

Koh-i-noor No. 5616 mechanical pencil (for lettering)

Rotary type pencil pointer

Dietzgen 3208 pencil pointer (sanding block)

Metal erasing shield

Electric eraser

Desk brush

Ruling pen, preferably spring-hinged

LeRoy, Unitech, or Wrico stylographic ink lettering set

Koh-i-noor Rapidograph ink pen set

Portable electric calculator

Addometer

4″ heavy-duty pen/pencil compass

Two or more French curves

Simplon flexible curve

Templates:

    RapiDesign No. 123 Isometric (ellipse)

    Dietzgen, True-Guide Circle, No. 2279

    Handy, Giant Circles, No. 201

    Cassell, Fixture Indicator, No. 103, $\frac{1}{8}$" scale

    RapiDesign No. 22 (revised)—for house plans

All triangles should be checked for accuracy. If a 90° triangle does not describe the same back-to-back line when "flip-flopped" along the same straight edge, the triangle should be discarded. For ink work, triangles with both edges beveled are particularly advantageous.

Every office needs to have all the time-saving drafting equipment and support equipment it can afford. Office needs will vary, but the essentials may include:

Whiteprint machine

Copy machine

Punching and binding machines

Electric typewriters

Dictating/transcribing units

Tape printout calculator

Polaroid camera

Surveyor's level and rod

Parallel drafting bar (one per drafting table)

Pantograph

Beam compass

12' tape measure

100' tape measure

Paper cutter

Normal and heavy-duty staplers

Special-use templates

Letter-size file cabinets

Flat files (for tracings in work)

Roll files (for tracings in storage)

Vertical plan holders (print clamps)

The whiteprint machine is an essential for even the smallest office. The convenience of being able to make a print immediately for reference, for tracing over, for unexpected conferences, and for evenings and weekends when the print shops are closed makes this unit indispensable to office efficiency. Another unit, nearly as essential, is the copying machine, which allows instant copying of small drawings, catalog pages, correspondence, and even specifications (if it is a large-capacity model).

Drafting supplies should be maintained in quantity and someone should be delegated to check weekly that an adequate amount of every item is on hand. A checklist is convenient for this inventory and for ordering the proper supplies.

PENCIL—OR INK

Common practice, as late as 25 years ago, was to produce the architectural drawings first in pencil, then trace them in ink on linen or vellum. Although examples of this practice may yet be found, the majority of architectural drawings today are produced directly on a fine-grade paper with pencil drawings and pencil lettering supplemented occasionally by ink where special bold emphasis is desired. The time necessary to produce the working drawings and the cost of labor involved makes the use of every practical, time-saving technique mandatory. Currently, efficiency favors pencil drawings for most projects, even in conjunction with many of photodrafting and other developing techniques (see Chapter 7). Therefore, the emphasis in this book will be on producing quality pencil drawings and lettering supplemented by ink only where added emphasis is desired.

PENCIL LEADS

By using leads of differing hardness, different weights (fineness, sharpness, or boldness) of line and lettering can be produced. However, keeping a different lead pencil handy for every change in line weight is time-consuming and unnecessary. Many superb draftors use only 2H and H pencil leads for drawing and lettering. By varying the pressure, one can learn to use 2H lead for most drawings, supplementing it with 3H lead for hatching (or hachuring) and dimension strings and with H lead for outlines (to improve the drawing's readability). H lead is suggested for all lettering. Leads harder than 3H are difficult to erase, and leads softer than H are easy to smear.

Drawing pencils may be sharpened in a rotary device or on a sandpaper pad; the latter method is preferred by those who wedge-sharpen the drawing pencil, as in Figure 3-4.

LINES

Figure 3-1 illustrates the types and weights of drawing lines. Tremendous differences can be effected by drawing with a very sharp pencil (for fineness) and by blunting the pencil (for boldness).

The quality of line weight and the technique of joining lines is further illustrated in Figure 3-2. General suggestions for improvement include:

1. Draw lines with uniform pressure throughout, including beginning and ending pressure, to avoid weakness at the ends.

2. Join straight lines to curves (including circles) by drawing the curve first and joining the straight line to it.

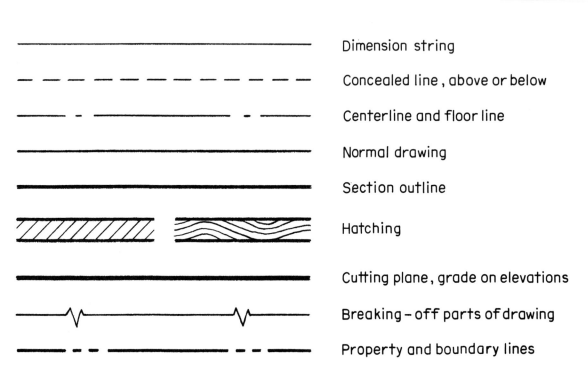

	Dimension string
	Concealed line, above or below
	Centerline and floor line
	Normal drawing
	Section outline
	Hatching
	Cutting plane, grade on elevations
	Breaking-off parts of drawing
	Property and boundary lines

FIGURE 3-1   LINE TYPES AND WEIGHTS.

(a) Good practice   (b) Unacceptable

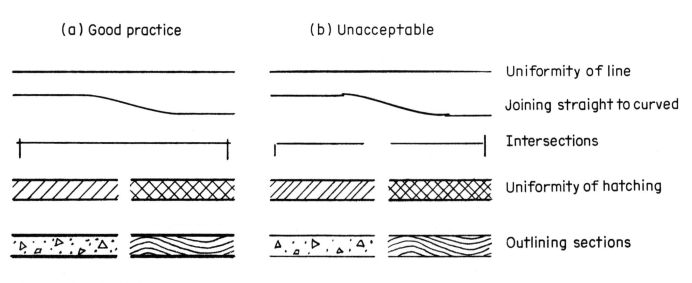

		Uniformity of line
		Joining straight to curved
		Intersections
		Uniformity of hatching
		Outlining sections

FIGURE 3-2   LINE DRAWING TECHNIQUES.

3. Run crossing lines through the corners (a minute distance) rather than drawing them to a point (which will often result in the lines actually stopping short of the point).

4. Make hatching uniform in weight and spacing.

5. Use a heavier. or bordering. outline around hatched materials or groups of materials.

Templates should be used to draw curves, ellipses, circles, squares, and other small geometrics and to draw plumbing fixtures and other complex small-scale figures. A bow compass should be used for drawing concentric circles and for inking circles.

IMPROVING THE READABILITY

In the·effort to increase the readability of the drawing, a heavy outline should describe the perimeter of the material in section, as illustrated in Figure 3-3, where two identical details are compared.

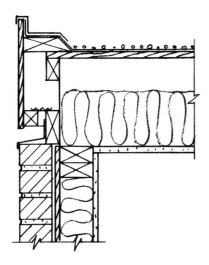

(a) Without outline

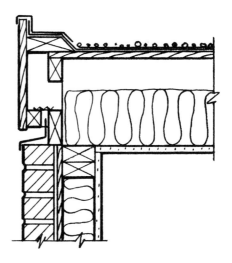

(b) With bold outline

FIGURE 3-3 OUTLINING THE SECTION.

Such outlining should follow both sides of all materials cut in section to give the visual effect that the heavily outlined materials are advancing from the drawing while the nonoutlined materials are receding. The readability of other drawings may be markedly improved by the heavy outlining of walls and partitions (in plan), the outlining of the perimeter of interior and exterior elevations, and the heavy bordering of property lines and buildings on the site plan. A heavy pencil line will be sufficient for most bordering, but an ink line may be necessary where exceptional clarity is important.

Occasionally the laminations of materials, such as a roofing membrane or plies of sheet metal, cannot be well illustrated without exaggerating the detail to show a separation of lines even when there will be no separation in the finished construction (as in the joining of coping and roofing in Figure 3-3). On occasion, a thin material such as sheet metal inserted between other materials, as in a flashing situation, can be better defined by being drawn in ink.

Protecting the readability of the drawing requires a good erasing technique. Various drafting papers, linens, and films will require different erasers, but the appropriate type used in an electric eraser can give good results quickly. A metal erasing shield should be used to prevent exposing more than the immediately affected area. In the case of removing a line, making a clean, sharp cutoff at each end, then erasing along the line, will minimize the smearing. A constant rotational movement of the erasing machine will help prevent burning through the drawing sheet.

DRAWING ACCURACY

Drawings must be made at precise scale. Small inaccuracies, accompanied by additional inaccuracies as a drawing develops, can result in such gross inaccuracies that minor or even major errors can result. Occasionally, (1) late changes may require some exaggeration to prevent the redrawing of the entire plan or detail and (2) some details may be illustrated at "no scale." These variances are not to be encouraged, but are acceptable if marked appropriately, as in "NTS" (not to scale). It is no great achievement for the professional draftor to produce the drawings at accurate scale; it is expected—it is mandatory. The mechanical and electrical consultants, working from the basic architectural drawings, are at a disadvantage in having to begin their drawings before all the changes have been included in the architectural drawings. Therefore, it is reasonable for them to include a drawing note (or preferably a specification clause) requiring the builder to scale only the architectural plans for locating fixtures and equipment, but this should not serve as an excuse for those consultants who fail to keep abreast of and account for the changes that will of necessity occur during the production of any architectural working drawings.

THE DRAWING TABLE AND THE STRAIGHTEDGE

There can be considerable debate on the pros and cons of drafting machines, parallel bars, and T squares as straightedges and on nearly vertical versus nearly flat tilt-tabletops; but the parallel bar on a slightly tilted table remains the preference of many when all concerns of accurate drawing and the placement of drawing tools and aids on or off the board are considered. However, for persons with back trouble or other physical difficulties, any position of the drawing board that is comfortable and any drawing aid that is needed should be provided.

The 72″ long drafting table is an optimum size for drafting in that it will accept a 48″ long parallel bar and allows adequate side spaces for scales, templates, and other paraphernalia. A tabletop overlay of off-white linoleum or ivory-tint resilient vinyl will make an excellent work surface. Some will prefer adding a roll tube, such as a Spiroll, at the lower edge to protect the bottom part of the sheet while the upper part is being worked on.

The parallel bar allows exceptional accuracy across the drawing face and, with practice, is easy to manipulate. Large (10″ or prefer-ably 12″) triangles allow greater accuracy for long lines and more flexibility for all drawing than small triangles. Engraving the angle degrees of standard roof pitches, such as $^6/_{12}$ = 26° 34′, etc., on an adjustable triangle will frequently save reference time.

HAND LETTERING

Despite all the available mechanical devices and reproduction processes, lettering remains largely a hand-produced process, and logically so, for architectural drawings are usually a further development of the design process, often original, seldom with a great amount of duplication from previous projects. Thus, the draw-ings require a highly adaptable lettering system that may follow every intricacy of the drawing layouts. It would be difficult to find anything as adaptable as hand lettering.

Titles *identify* the drawing, and the notes are meant to *explain* it, *not compete* with it. Thus the lettering must be simple and well formed to be easily read. Loops, such as those in 4, 6, 8, 9, B, P, etc., must be kept very open or they will appear closed up when reproduced.

Figure 3-4 presents four appropriate styles of lettering that are simple to form and easy to read. *Vertical* lettering is more compati-ble with the right-angle appearance of most drawings and is espe-cially preferable for presentation drawings. However, uniformity among draftors may be easier to achieve with *inclined* lettering—the effort may be less fatiguing for right-handers and the effect is very acceptable for working drawings. For letters of equal height, *uppercase* figures allow more openness and therefore better read-ability when reproduced and so are preferred for reduced-size reproduction; they also require only two guidelines. Carefully formed *lowercase* letters are acceptable in many cases, and will be required to designate many metric symbols. For uniformity, each office should designate a lettering style for its entire produc-

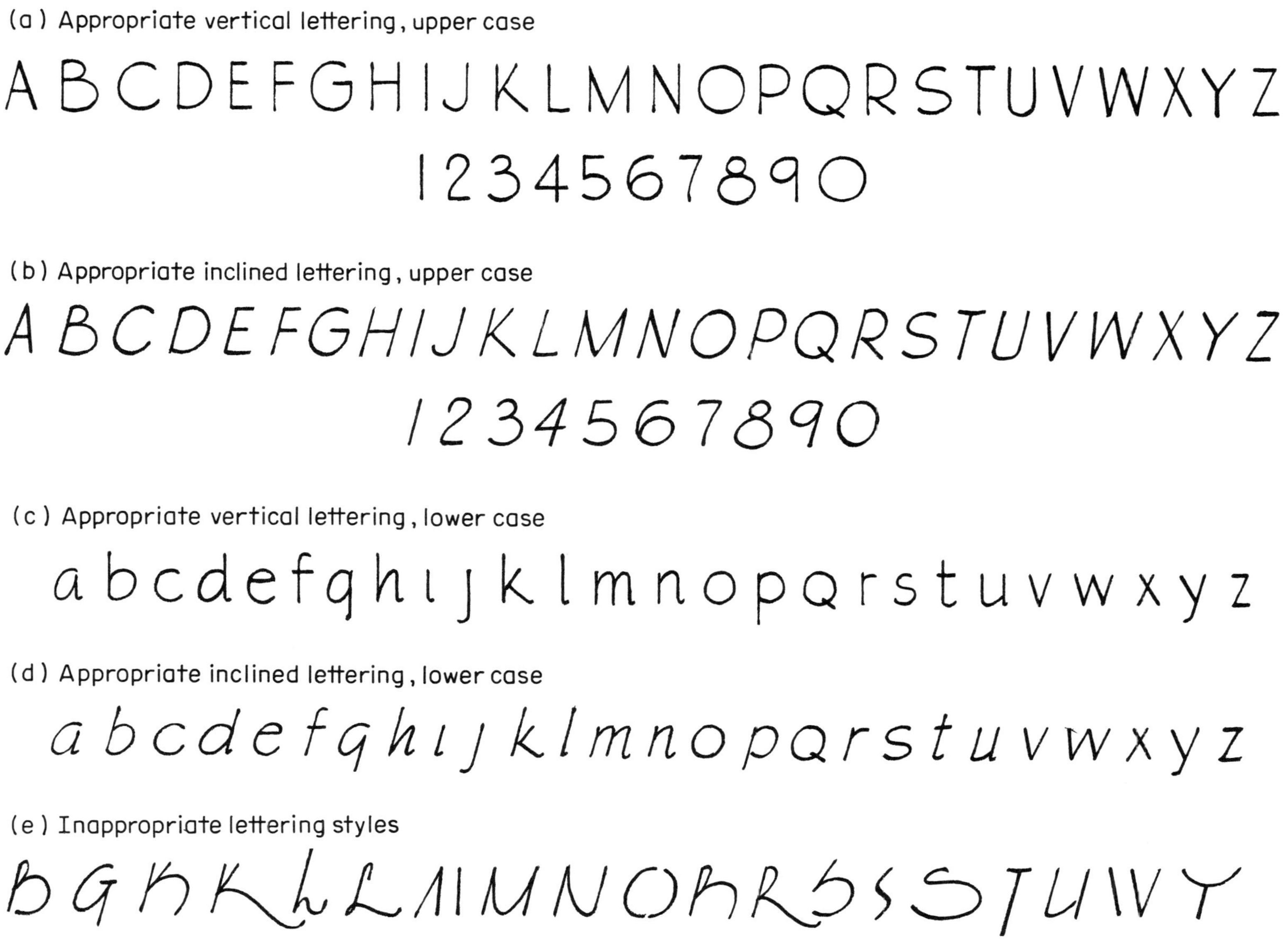

(a) Appropriate vertical lettering, upper case

ABCDEFGHIJKLMNOPQRSTUVWXYZ
1234567890

(b) Appropriate inclined lettering, upper case

ABCDEFGHIJKLMNOPQRSTUVWXYZ
1234567890

(c) Appropriate vertical lettering, lower case

abcdefghijklmnopqrstuvwxyz

(d) Appropriate inclined lettering, lower case

abcdefghijklmnopqrstuvwxyz

(e) Inappropriate lettering styles

bghkℓℒℳNOPℛbsSTUVY

FIGURE 3-4   HAND LETTERING STYLES.

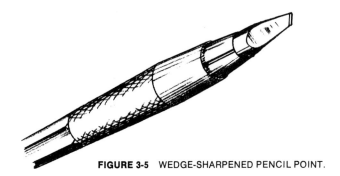

FIGURE 3-5   WEDGE-SHARPENED PENCIL POINT.

tion staff. Reading a sheet of drawings on which several draftors have worked and finding an equal number of distinctly different lettering styles is disconcerting. An accomplished draftor should have no problem in using any of these basic lettering styles. Stylized letters, as in Figure 3-4e, are simply not appropriate; they call attention to the lettering rather than to the drawing.

Shaded letters (thick-and-thin) can add readability and esthetics. The pencil lead is sharpened first in the round, then quickly whetted on each side on a sandpaper pad to form a wedge-like point, as in Figure 3-5. The pencil is then held with the long dimension of the point in the vertical or inclined direction (depending on the letter style); the point acts much like the runner of a sled, giving a fine line in one direction and a broad line in the other. The sled-runner-effect aids the hand in drawing a straighter vertical or inclined line and thereby can improve the lettering; conversely, a round point tends to follow every undulation of the hand and of the paper.

Learning to form letters well and rapidly is a matter of self-discipline and diligent practice. A half hour of concentrated lettering practice each day over as short a time as two or three weeks can dramatically improve lettering technique and speed of execution. The draftor should not resort to the use of such time-consuming crutches as triangles and straightedges for letter alignment and uniformity.

Figure 3-6 suggests several practice routines and methods to improve the form of the letters. As the golfer improves his or her

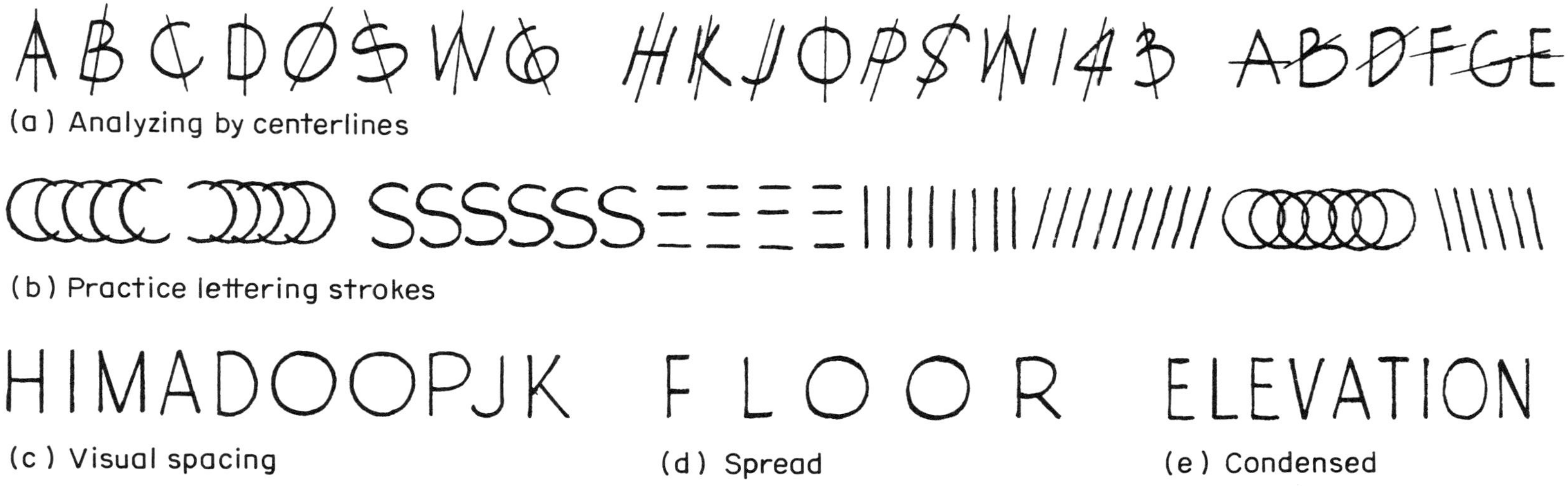

A B C D S W (a) Analyzing by centerlines

H K J O P S W 14 B   A B D F G E

S S S S S S ≡ ≡ ≡ ≡ ||||||| /////// ⊙⊙⊙⊙⊙ \\\\\\\

(b) Practice lettering strokes

H I M A D O O P J K   F L O O R   E L E V A T I O N

(c) Visual spacing   (d) Spread   (e) Condensed

FIGURE 3-6   ANALYSIS OF THE LETTERING.

game by practicing strokes on the driving range and putting green, so the draftor should seek to improve his or her lettering by practicing letter strokes rather than concentrating wholly on the letters themselves. Drawing a series of parallel, vertical, inclined, and horizontal lines and a series of half circles, etc., will improve the basic stroke by allowing concentration on those particular hand movements. The Speedball Textbooks are an excellent reference for learning basic lettering strokes and styles.

Each letter and number should be quickly formed by one continuous stroke of the pencil. There should be uniformity of letter style (all S's should be formed similarly, etc.). A lack of alignment (vertical, inclined, or horizontal) will become apparent by comparing lines drawn through the *visual* centers of the letters, as in Figure 3-6a. When the letters are properly formed, all the visual centerlines should be parallel. The spacing of the letters should be done visually rather than mechanically, which will result in differences in spacing when curved, inclined, and vertical letters are set in different relationships. Variety in spacing can aid the effect of the graphics on the drawing. But whether the letters are spaced normally, or are spread or condensed, the closest spacing interval will be between back-to-back circular forms and the widest spacing between parallel lines, with other forms adjusted accordingly (see Figure 3-6c, d, and e). By practicing lettering strokes in series, as in Figure 3-6b, the uniformity of spacing and of line, or the lack thereof, can be easily observed. Finally, each practice sheet should be tested by running it through the reproduction machine, for the end result is to exhibit lettering that is well formed and easily read when reproduced.

LETTERING SIZE

Although it is not always possible, an effort should be made to achieve general uniformity in the size of lettering in each set of drawings—one uniform size for titles, another for subtitles, another for normal notes, etc. The scale of the drawing, the size of the space, and the conflict between the lettering and other drawing elements will frequently require adjustment in the size of the lettering to maintain clarity and visual compatibility. Figure 3-7 shows two details in which the visual aspects of lettering uniformity and the importance of being *in scale* with the drawing are apparent.

In the production of drawings scaled at $\frac{1}{8}'' = 1'-0''$, the following spacing of guidelines for uppercase letters will usually give good results:

Fractional Inch	Lettering Guide Number	Use
$\frac{7}{32}$	7	Titles of plans, details, schedules
$\frac{5}{32}$	5	Titles of subdetails
$\frac{1}{8}$	4	Room names
$\frac{7}{64}$	$3\frac{1}{2}$	Dimensions and normal notes
$\frac{5}{64}$	$2\frac{1}{2}$	Smallest notes

Uniform-height lettering requires lightly drawn guidelines, never heavy enough to show in the reproduction. An adjustable lettering guide is convenient for this purpose, but it can also become a crutch. Many draftors learn to "eyeball" the guidelines with considerable accuracy, and this practice can make the draftor more aware of the need to occasionally change the size of the lettering due to the scale of the drawing.

When drawings will be reproduced at a smaller size, the lettering must be commensurately larger. For 50 percent reduction, the smallest element of the original hand lettering should not be less than $\frac{1}{8}''$ for uppercase or $\frac{5}{32}''$ for lowercase guidelines, but the real test is how readable the lettering becomes after reproduction. Certain agencies, such as the U.S. Corps of Engineers, have detailed requirements for the size of the lettering used in their

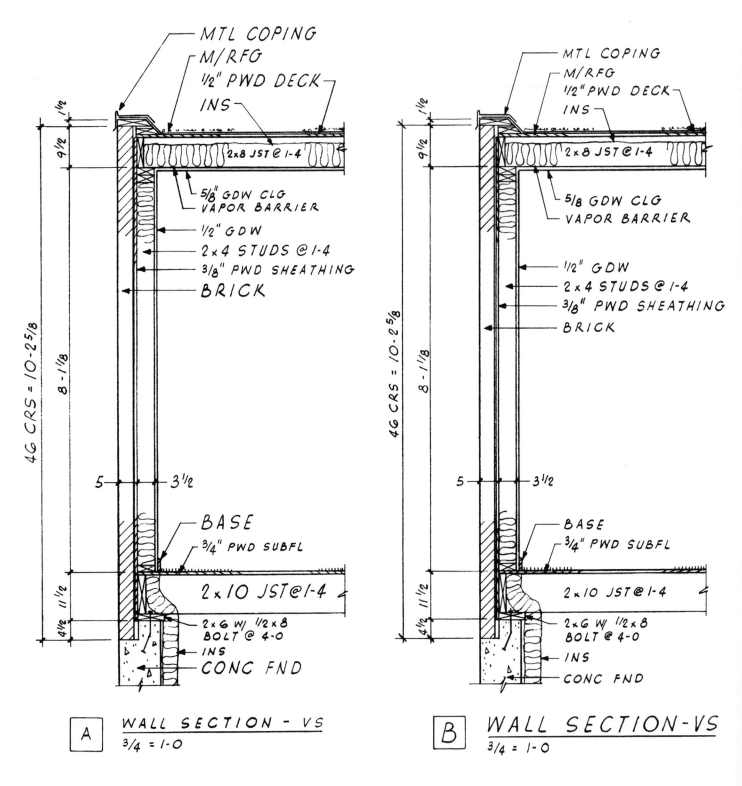

FIGURE 3-7   LETTERING-SIZE UNIFORMITY, *IN SCALE* WITH THE DRAWING.

contract documents. Many construction documents are microfilmed for bidding, such as in the Dodge/SCAN service for contractors and subcontractors, and users will be unable to decipher the notes unless the lettering on the original drawing is simple and of adequate size for the photoreduction process.

Lettering aids are available, such as stylographic inking pens, transfer (press-on) lettering, and special long-carriage typewriters. Titles and notes of various sizes and of great uniformity can be provided with these aids; however, they require greater care in planning and lettering arrangement than hand lettering, and some may require greater execution time.

DRAWINGS NOTES

Organizing the notes on the drawing by grouping related notes, as in Figure 3-8, and by using vertical alignment, as in Figure 3-7, will improve both the clarity and the esthetics. The notes should be added immediately upon completing the drawing while the carefully worked out information is still in mind.

The note must be arrowed to the item or material being described with an indication string terminating with an arrowhead. The point of the arrowhead should generally terminate on the material or surface, but placing the arrowhead within the body of the material, or near it, may frequently be necessary to avoid interference with other lines or material indications. The arrowhead should be made *in scale* with the drawings and of the types indicated in Figure 3-9. The arrow string *and the arrowhead* should *always* be added at the same time as the note so they will not be forgotten.

Real savings in time and improvement in clarity are possible by structuring the drawing notes to be as definite and as brief as possible. Words such as "all," "shall," and "shall be" can be eliminated. Normally, notes need only call out the material and its specifics. Where further instructions are necessary, the note should

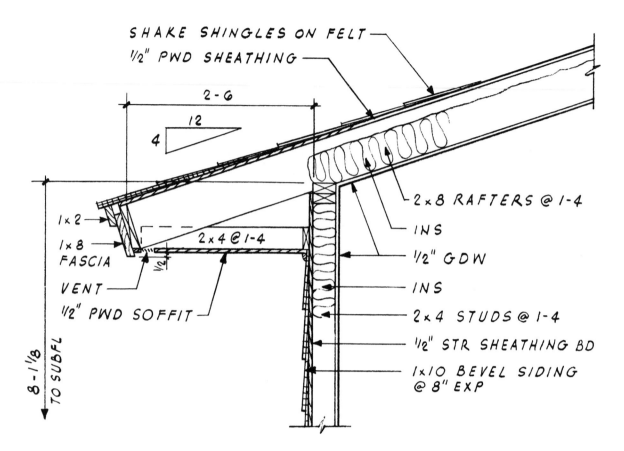

SHAKE SHINGLES ON FELT

½" PWD SHEATHING

2 - 6

12

4

1 x 2

1 x 8
FASCIA

VENT

½" PWD SOFFIT

½

2 x 4 @ 1-4

2 x 8 RAFTERS @ 1-4

INS

½" GDW

INS

2 x 4 STUDS @ 1-4

½" STR SHEATHING BD

1 x 10 BEVEL SIDING
@ 8" EXP

8 - 1⅛
TO SUBFL

FIGURE 3-8 ORGANIZING THE DRAWING NOTES.

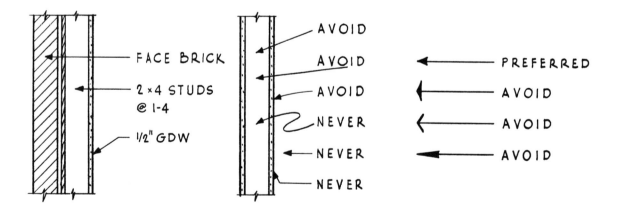

FACE BRICK

2 x 4 STUDS
@ 1-4

½" GDW

AVOID

AVOID

AVOID

NEVER

NEVER

NEVER

PREFERRED

AVOID

AVOID

AVOID

FIGURE 3-9 ARROWS AND ARROWHEADS.

be a directive to the builder stated in the *imperative case* (setting the verb first), such as "Remove brick cornice," "Rake vertical joints," or "Weld corners and grind smooth." The following revisions of typical notes serve as other examples of preferred brevity:

Original Note	*As Revised*
Contractor shall provide weep holes at 24″ o.c.	Weeps @ 2-0
All slabs shall be reinforced with 6 × 6-1010 welded wire fabric	6 × 6-1010 WWF
Furnish and install precast concrete panels	PCC panels
Remove existing metal door and provide new metal door	Replace mtl door

These additional general rules should be observed in making notes on the drawings:

1. *Know the specifications.* Don't describe something that will obviously be described in the specifications.

2. Let the specifications identify the specifics of a material. Thus the drawing note may read "1 × 6 T&G Soffit," and let the specifications identify it as pine or fir, etc.

3. Name each material by its use so that the specifications can identify it by the same term; for example: 1 × 8 facia, ½″ pwd sheathing, 1 × 10 bevel siding.

4. Avoid noting "see specs," which is normally redundant since it is fundamental that the builder refer to the specifications.

5. Avoid phrases requiring the work to be "new" or to be "furnished and installed." These phrases become redundant when the specifications general conditions require all materials be new and that they be furnished and installed.

6. Don't note "see detail" or "see site plan"; instead, follow the identification by a boxed reference number; for example, FIREPLACE 2B1 identifies precisely where the detail may be found. If the reference

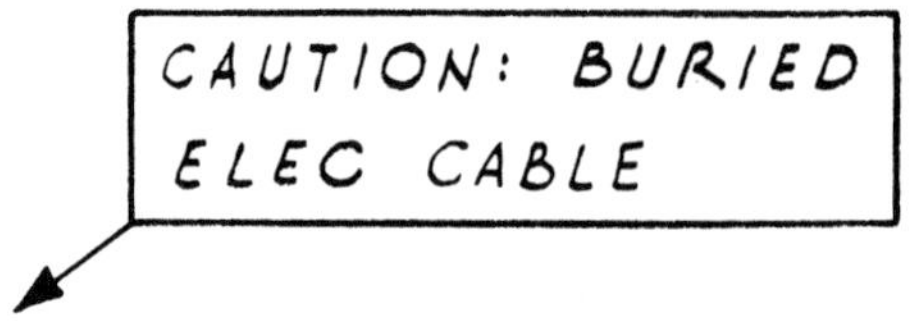

CAUTION: BURIED
ELEC CABLE

FIGURE 3-10   BOXING A NOTE FOR EMPHASIS.

location is not known at the time of the initial drawing, draw the blank box, which will call attention to the fact that it must be filled in later.

7. Avoid using the word "detail" in notes and titles. Most details are horizontal or vertical sections and should be identified as such.

8. Avoid excessive repetition of notes on elevations, plans, and sections. A brick wall, indicated once by noting or by hatching, is still a brick wall farther on.

9. Pencil in a large rough X in the space when a note cannot be completed at the time, thereby calling attention to the missing note.

10. Indicate equipment with a dotted line and identify it, as in Figure 2-7, when it is not a part of the contract but when the size and location is important for reference. Use the letters "NIC" to identify equipment or items not included in the construction contract.

11. "Box" a very important note to call attention to it (see Figure 3-10).

4

DIMENSIONING

4 | DIMENSIONING

Accurate dimensioning is an unqualified must! The dimension the draftor establishes will be used by many others in laying out the building, fabricating products, and assembling components, but unfortunately, the draftor may not have the opportunity to discover an error until the construction is so far along that a correction will prove costly—to someone. Therefore, there is no margin for error and no excuse for making an error. The draftor must adopt a systematic discipline for establishing the dimensions and an equally systematic discipline for checking and rechecking them.

DIMENSIONAL EXPRESSIONS

Figure 4-1 presents a system of dimensional expressions that promotes brevity by eliminating foot and inch marks in the majority of cases; it also illustrates the relationship of modular dimensions to walls and partitions. Figure 4-1 is shown as an appendix sheet of the specifications, thereby serving as a reference to all the drawing disciplines without needing to appear on the drawing sheets. To complete the reference, a *boxed* note should be placed on drawings directing attention to the appendix. Alternatively, the same information might be printed or copied on transfer film and affixed to the drawing sheet rather than appearing in the specifications.

DIMENSION STRINGS

Although the terminal points of the dimension string can be made by arrows or dots, a bold diagonal cross is the quickest to execute. The dimensions are normally written above the dimension string. However, an improvised placement of the dimensions will frequently be required for clarity where space is limited. A careful arrangement of interior dimension strings can avoid conflicts between dimensions and other plan elements, as in Figure 4-2. Generally, a dimension should not occur within a wall or partition.

DIMENSIONAL EXPRESSIONS   APPENDIX AP4

DIMENSIONS WITH FOOT & INCH MARKS OMITTED:
UNIFIED NUMBERS LESS THAN 12 INDICATE INCHES, AS... $11^{3}/_{4}$
HYPHENATED NUMBERS 1-0 AND OVER INDICATE FEET AND INCHES, AS...$2-1^{1}/_{2}$

FOOT & INCH MARKS NOT USED:
WITH A DIMENSION STRING, AS... $20-0^{1}/_{2}$ OR... $^{3}/_{8}$
WITH AN INDICATION OF SCALE, AS... $^{3}/_{4}=1-0$, OR...SCALE ELEVATIONS: $^{1}/_{4}=1-0$
WITH AN ELEVATION RELATED TO DATUM, AS... EL $102-2^{1}/_{4}$
WITH A DRAWING NOTE USING FEET AND INCHES, AS... 2-6 x 1-8 ACCESS
WITH A DRAWING NOTE USING STANDARD COMBINATIONS FOR MATERIALS,
    AS...2x6 RAFTERS @ 1-4, OR FOR A STEEL ANGLE, AS...$\angle 4 \times 4 \times ^{3}/_{8} \times 4-8$

FOOT & INCH MARKS ARE USED:
WITH A DRAWING NOTE USING INCHES ONLY, AS... $^{1}/_{2}$" BOLT, OR...$^{3}/_{4}$" PLYWOOD

FEET AND DECIMALS OF A FOOT ARE USED ON SITE PLANS:
FOR GRADE CONTOURS, AS... — 96 — EXISTING, OR... 98 FINISH
FOR SPOT FINISH GRADES, AS... 98.7, OR EXISTING GRADE, AS... 96.2
FOR BOUNDARY DIMENSIONS, AS... 725.14'

DIMENSIONS FOR WALLS AND PARTITIONS ARE MODULAR RATHER THAN ACTUAL. THESE DETAILS ARE TYPICAL:

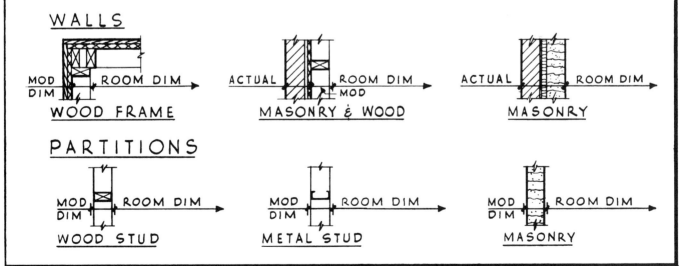

FIGURE 4-1 DIMENSIONAL EXPRESSIONS (AS APPEARING IN THE SPECIFICATIONS APPENDIX).

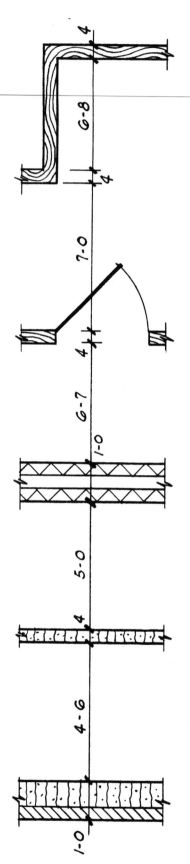

FIGURE 4-2 DIMENSIONING WALLS AND PARTITIONS IN PLAN.

RELATING THE DIMENSIONS TO THE STRUCTURE

The plan dimensioning begins with the critical spaces or structural elements, which are usually designated on the main floor plan. This floor plan is dimensioned first and is followed by other floor and foundation plans with dimensions carefully coordinated to it. In construction, the structural elements (such as walls, columns, beams, etc.) are framed before the finish work is placed, so *the basic dimension must be to the structure* for both horizontal and vertical components. The finish will not be accurate unless the structure is dimensionally controlled.

For buildings of wall-bearing construction, the exterior dimensions of the floor plan can generally be arranged in a manner similar to that in Figure 4-3 in which three basic dimension strings are used: (1) for overall dimensions, (2) for major offsets in the wall configuration, and (3) for openings in the walls. Additional dimension strings may be required for special items. This arrangement permits systematic checking in that the dimensions along the *opening* string must total that of the *offset* string for the given wall length, and the individual wall lengths, or *offsets,* must total the *overall* dimension. The parenthesized dimensions illustrate a method of expressing metric equivalents during the "metric transition period" (see Chapter 5).

In structurally framed buildings, the columns must be dimensioned, and the column lines should be numbered, as in Figure 4-4, in order to relate them to structural schedules and other identifications.

In multistory buildings the concrete columns may vary in size by floors. Therefore, the dimensioning should be to the column face wherever that face must be controlled; otherwise the dimensioning should be to the centerline (see Figure 4-5). Except where dimensional control from a column face is necessary, steel columns should be dimensioned to their centerlines. Although in most framed buildings the columns are numbered consecutively in one direction and alphabetically in the other, in very simple buildings

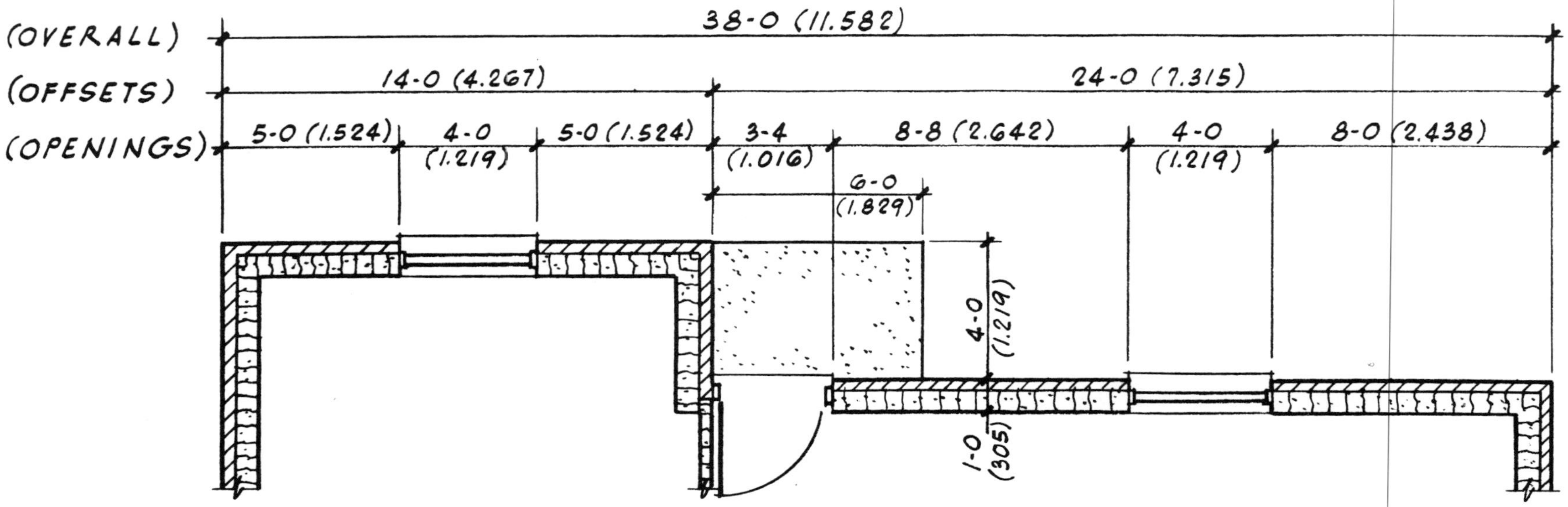

FIGURE 4-3 EXTERIOR DIMENSIONING SYSTEM FOR WALL-BEARING CONSTRUCTION.

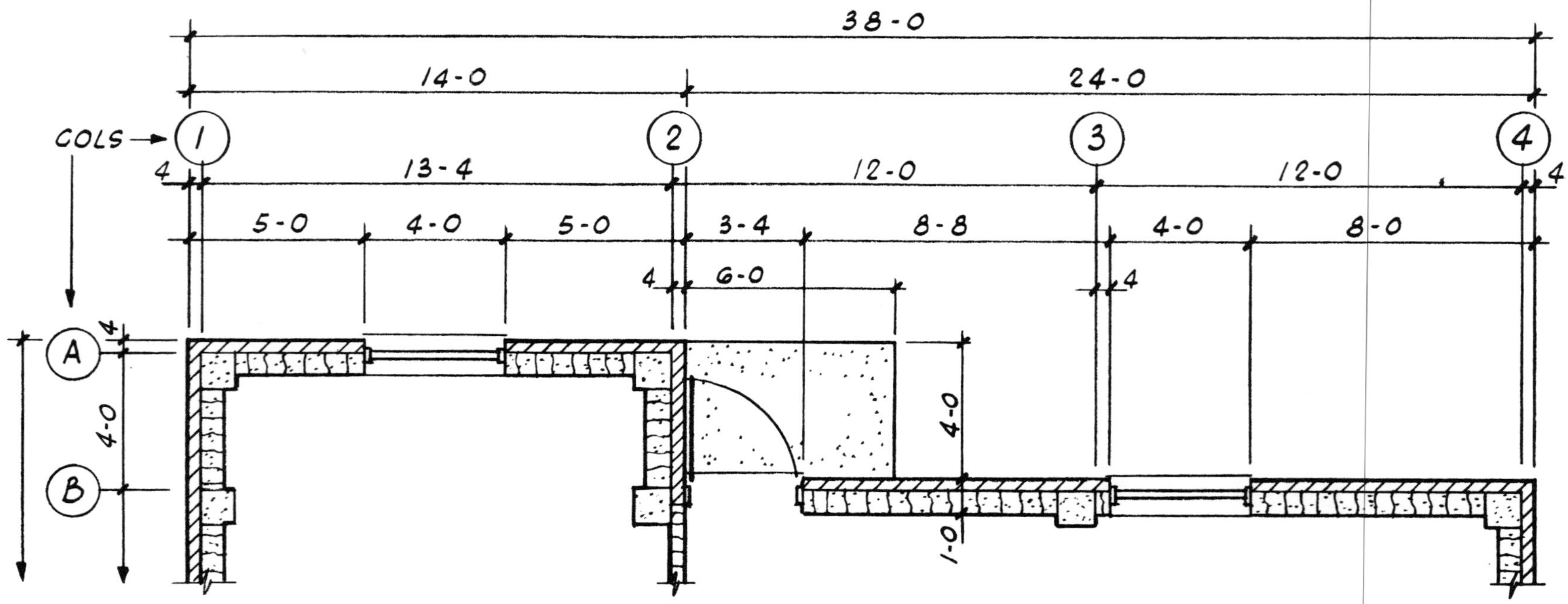

FIGURE 4-4 EXTERIOR DIMENSIONING SYSTEM WITH COLUMNS.

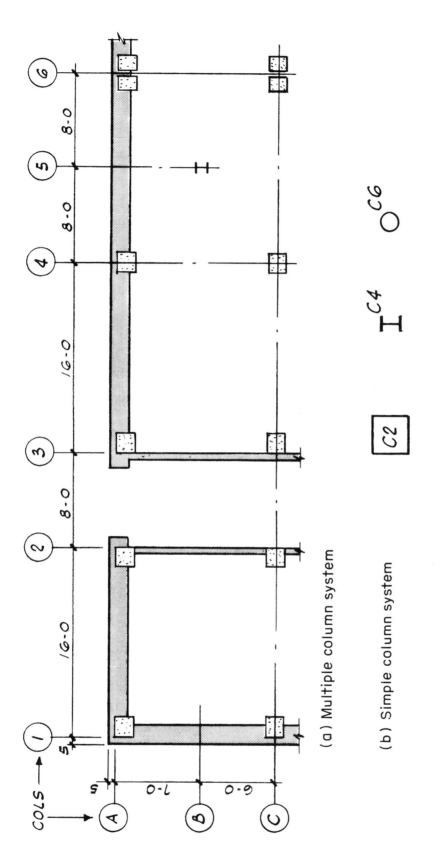

(a) Multiple column system

(b) Simple column system

FIGURE 4-5 COLUMN IDENTIFICATION SYSTEMS.

75

with few columns it may be convenient to number them as indicated in Figure 4-5*b*.

The dimensioning system must also relate vertically to the structure, as in Figure 4-6, where two basic types of wall construction are shown. The basic dimensioning identifies the critical structural

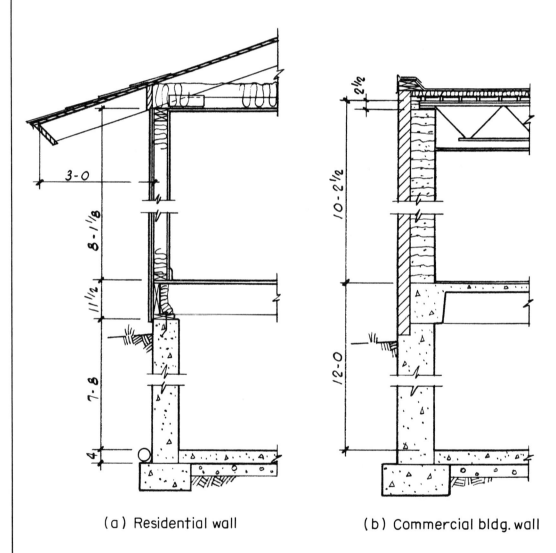

(a) Residential wall   (b) Commercial bldg. wall

FIGURE 4-6 VERTICAL DIMENSIONS RELATED TO THE STRUCTURE.

points, such as the top of footing, top of slab, top of concrete wall, top of subfloor, and top of wall plates (bottom of ceiling joists) in (a), and the top of concrete floor slabs and top of structural steel in (b). Other dimensions may be added, all relating to this basic structural reference. Arranging the dimensions on the left of the vertical section will allow developing the notes on the right later.

MODULAR DIMENSIONING

A building-dimensioning system based on multiples of the 4″ module will complement the use of such modular construction units as concrete blocks, bricks, and plywood. Used as a nominal dimensioning system, as in Figure 4-1, the system is very practical, although it becomes far too complicated for most architects and builders if used in its purest sense (a grid in space with actual materials dimensioned from the grid by a system of dots and arrows). In the nominal floor plan system, the dimensioning recognizes the actual face of the exterior wall and the control face or the centerlines of columns but uses a nominal dimension for the thickness of walls and partitions (see Figure 4-1), openings in walls, etc. Although there is some imprecision, the differences are well within the tolerances for most building construction, and the advantage of relating to 4″ and larger modules (eliminating most fractional inches) is a distinct asset for both the draftor and the builder in establishing and later checking the dimensions.

Figure 4-7a shows the modular grid system applied to the floor plan of a building of wall-bearing construction, while Figure 4-7b shows it applied to the floor plan of a structure supported by columns. The basic difference is in the numbering of the grid lines. In Figure 4-7a the grid numbers in each direction also describe the dimensions in feet from grid 0. In Figure 4-7b the same feature of describing the grid dimension in feet is maintained, but an orientation letter is added (W for west, N for north, etc.) in order to identify the column lines, especially for the schedules where numbering such as 32N/16W would be used.

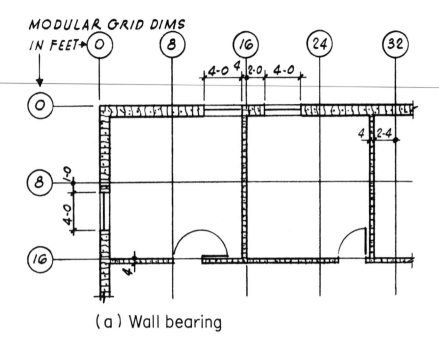

(a) Wall bearing

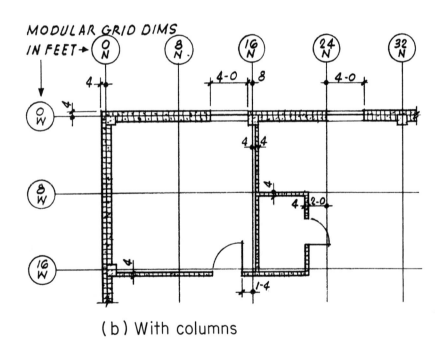

(b) With columns

FIGURE 4-7 MODULAR PLAN DIMENSIONS.

Drawing papers and films are available bearing a preprinted, nonreproducing grid which can assist in maintaining a modular control on the lengths and spacing of the construction units while the floor plans are being developed. Those grids which are to appear in the reproduction must be traced, preferably on the back of the sheet to avoid being erased as changes are made. Windows and doors, interior partitions, and other elements can be conveniently located from the nearest grid rather than by lengthy dimension strings outside and inside the building. Although the concept may lead one to presuppose that once the floor diaphragms are in place the grid can be struck on the floors as a guide to laying out walls and partitions, this is seldom practical. However, the ability to dimensionally locate any element from a grid station at a physical wall or structural element is quite workable.

DIMENSIONING OPENINGS, IN PLAN

In wood-framed walls, dimensioning windows and doors to the centerlines is advisable, as in Figure 4-8a. Manufacturer's shop drawings will give the framing openings sizes required, and if a substitution is permitted for another manufacturer's window, the opening difference will not result in a different center-to-center spacing between openings.

In masonry walls, the masonry opening dimension of windows, doors, and other openings should be given, as in Figure 4-8b. The dimensions should account for the laying lengths of the masonry units to avoid excessive cutting, where possible. Units such as steel doorframes are usually built in as the masonry is laid, and therefore the opening dimension is expressed in the actual out-to-out dimension of the frame, and the end joints of the masonry are correspondingly adjusted.

The precise location of a door or other opening in a partition should be dimensioned when the location is important. Otherwise, the dimension can be left to the builder's scale interpretation, thereby allowing reasonable adjustment in the position to avoid unnecessary cutting of masonry units or respacing of studs.

DIMENSION-CONTROL DIAGRAMS

Complicated structures require special dimensional control. In the case of an angular floor plan, an angle diagram establishes the baselines, working points, and the basic layout dimensions; it will assist in the dimensioning during the preparation of drawings; and it will be of fundamental assistance to the builder in making an accurate building layout in the field (see Figure 4-9). The diagram should be drawn adjacent to the floor plan.

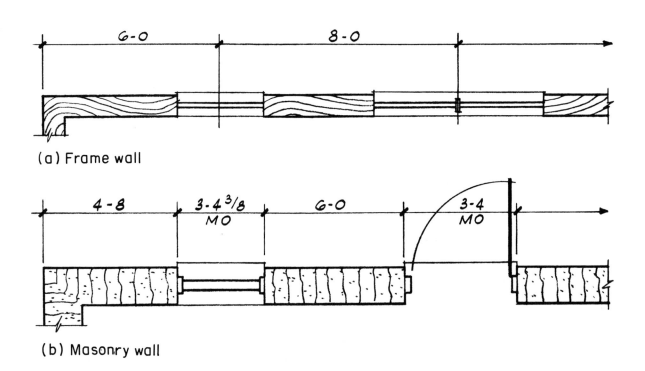

(a) Frame wall

(b) Masonry wall

FIGURE 4-8 DIMENSIONING WINDOWS AND DOORS IN PLAN.

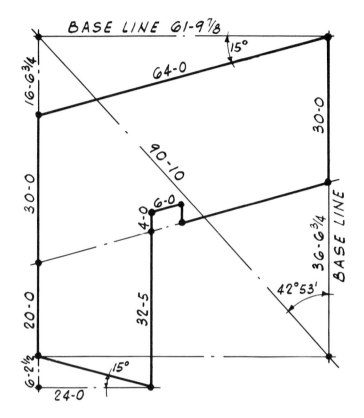

FIGURE 4-9 FLOOR PLAN DIMENSION-CONTROL DIAGRAM.

For a complex floor- and roof-framing system, a vertical cross section through the building should be drawn in line diagram, as in Figure 4-10, at the largest practical scale and with all conditions projected into a single drawing plane where all basic dimensions and working points can be established. This drawing must be made with precision so that the dimensions may be checked by scale; the angular dimensions should be further checked by trigonometry or by Smoley's Tables. Although this vertical dimension-control diagram will not appear on the drawings, it should be

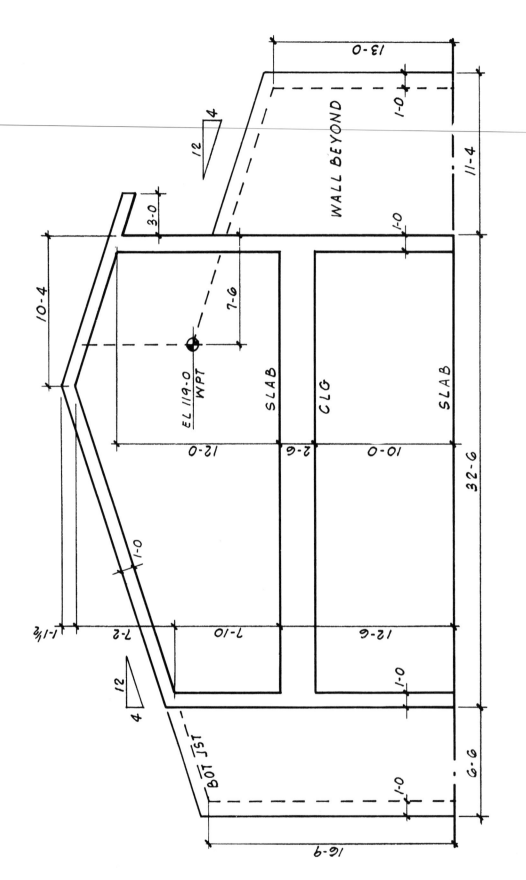

FIGURE 4-10 VERTICAL DIMENSION-CONTROL DIAGRAM.

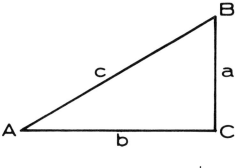

$$\sin A = \frac{a}{c} \qquad \cos A = \frac{b}{c}$$

$$\tan A = \frac{a}{b} \qquad \cot A = \frac{b}{a}$$

$$\sec A = \frac{c}{b} \qquad \csc A = \frac{c}{a}$$

FIGURE 4-11   BASIC TRIGONOMETRIC
FUNCTIONS OF ANGLE *A*.

retained to serve as a reference during the further development of vertical dimensioning and during the construction period.

Reproductions of all dimension-control diagrams should be made available to the structural engineer as an assistance in coordinating the structural dimensions.

Figure 4-11 presents the six basic trigonometric functions of an angle as a quick reference in beginning the solution to an angular diagram. Referring to a mathematical textbook or a handbook with natural trigonometric functions should give the additional tabular information for solving any of the angles or sides of the triangle.

DIMENSIONS EXPRESSED AS ELEVATIONS

Using elevations in reference to the building datum is convenient as a supplement to the vertical dimensioning systems. These ele-

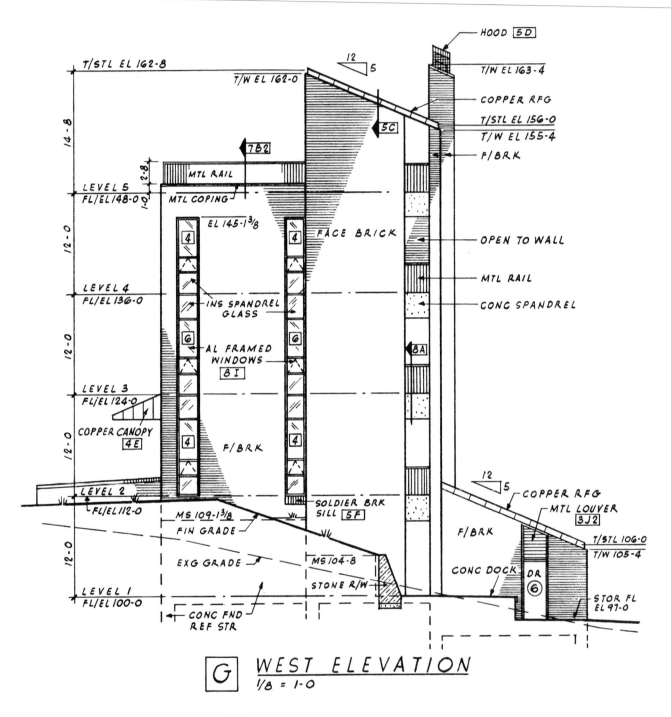

FIGURE 4-12 EXTERIOR ELEVATION.

vations can be recorded on the exterior elevations, as in Figure 4-12, on the floor plans, as in Figure 6-7, or in details where dimension strings cannot be extended to floor lines or to other framing. These elevations must be expressed in feet and inches for the building components and for the exterior elements such as stairs, ramps, docks, and platforms directly attached to the building.

MISCELLANEOUS DIMENSIONING

When the ceiling is suspended by a grid framing system, that grid should be drawn as a reflected ceiling plan, as in Figure 4-13, properly located from the interior walls and columns. The ceiling grid should also be related to the modular grid system if such is used. The drawing should indicate partitions extending through the ceiling system and should indicate the different ceiling materials and all changes in levels. Drawing the reflected ceiling plan in the early development stages can assist those preparing the mechanical and electrical layouts by coordinating the locations of light fixtures and registers.

Figure 4-14 illustrates several examples of dimensions that are conveyed by special symbols or notations. The standard AISC designations for structural steel are given because they are so frequently used in the architectural and structural drawings—and are frequently designated incorrectly. As with all products, the standard industry designations should be used.

SITE DIMENSIONS

For the convenience of converting rod readings, for graphing slopes, and for calculating the cut and fill of earthwork, topographic site elevations are usually recorded in feet and tenths of feet, as in 899.6, 905.4, etc. (see Figure 4-1). These site elevations are usually established in reference to sea level or to a temporary site datum (which must be identified), while the building drawings

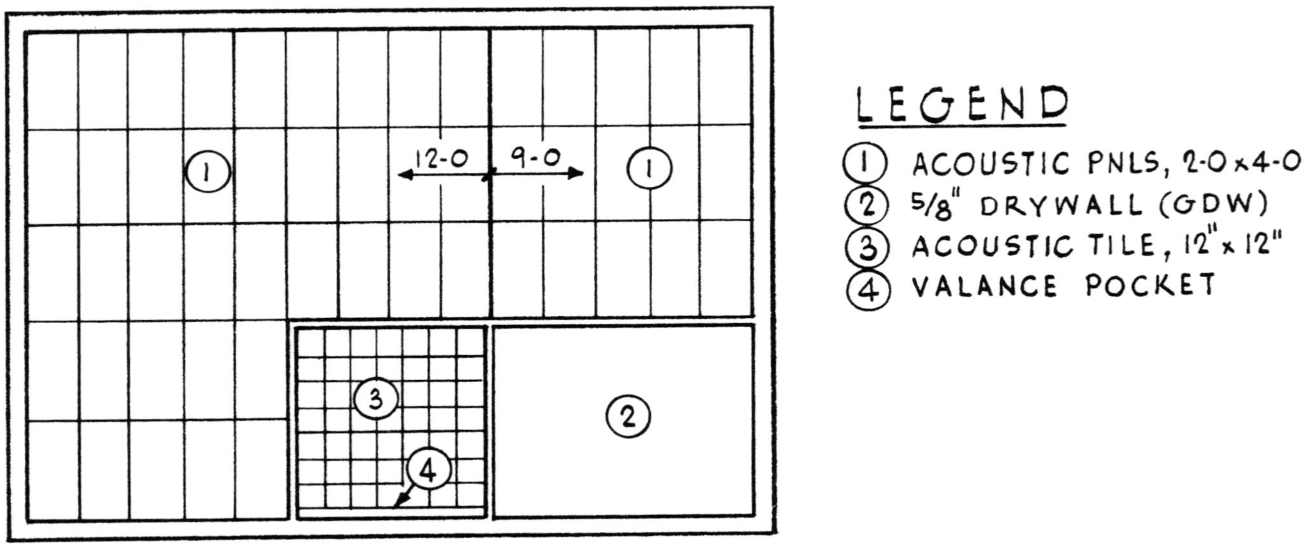

LEGEND

1. ACOUSTIC PNLS, 2-0 x 4-0
2. 5/8" DRYWALL (GDW)
3. ACOUSTIC TILE, 12" x 12"
4. VALANCE POCKET

FIGURE 4-13 REFLECTED CEILING PLAN.

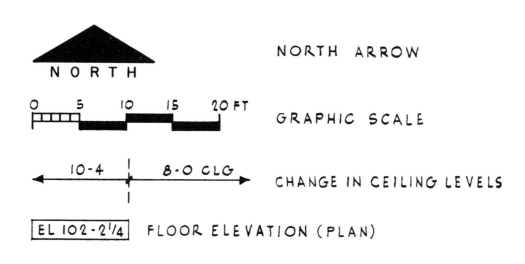

NORTH ARROW

GRAPHIC SCALE

CHANGE IN CEILING LEVELS

FLOOR ELEVATION (PLAN)

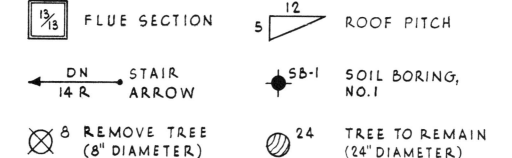

FLUE SECTION

ROOF PITCH

STAIR ARROW

SOIL BORING, NO.1

REMOVE TREE (8" DIAMETER)

TREE TO REMAIN (24" DIAMETER)

TYPICAL DESIGNATIONS FOR STEEL SECTIONS

W 8 x 40	W SHAPE
M 8 x 18.5	M SHAPE
∠ 6 x 4 x ⅝ LLV	UNEQUAL LEG ANGLE, LONG LEG VERTICAL
C 12 x 20.7	AMERICAN STANDARD CHANNEL
PIPE 4 STD	PIPE
TS 5 x 5 x .375	STRUCTURAL TUBING, SQUARE
PL ½ x 10	PLATE
BAR 1¼ □	SQUARE BAR
BAR 1¼ ⌀	ROUND BAR
BAR 2½ x ½	FLAT BAR

FIGURE 4-14 SPECIAL DIMENSIONS, SYMBOLS, AND NOTATIONS.

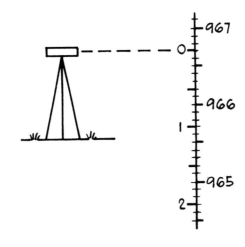

FIGURE 4-15 CONVERTING SITE ROD
READINGS TO DATUM.

will be related to floor levels or other building datum. This relationship between the building datum and the site datum must be
recorded on the site plan and preferably again on the main floor
plan with a note such as "Building Elevation 100-0 = Site Elevation
932.3." Construction conditions frequently require adjustment of
the building elevation, up or down, and this will obviously affect the
levels of slabs, docks, platforms, planter walls, and other elements
directly attached to the building. Therefore, these attached elements should be indicated by building elevations rather than by
site elevations.

Draftors are frequently concerned with converting and coordinating field elevations with final site elevations. Field elevations are
normally made by using a level instrument and a rod; rod readings
are recorded inversely (the lower the terrain, the larger the rod
reading), and therefore must be converted to coincide with a bench
mark or sea-level datum reference. The mental arithmetic gymnas-
tics of this conversion can be avoided by making a vertical line

graph at any convenient scale recording the field rod readings on the left and the sea-level elevations on the right, as in Figure 4-15, where field rod reading 1.0' (below eye piece) = sea-level elevation 965.7'. Once this initial relationship is graphically set, all other site rod readings can be instantly converted to sea-level elevations by direct readings from the line graph.

5

THE METRIC
SYSTEM

GOING METRIC

The Metric Conversion Act of 1975 committed the United States to a conversion to the metric system of measures. The conversion will be time-consuming and costly and can only be successfully achieved in the building industry—a fragmented giant with no central coordinating head—through a coordinated effort.

No realistic date has yet been set in the United States for "M-Day" (the date of achieving full metric conversion). Several areas of the construction industry have made their conversion commitments; many have not. Several large segments of American industry, including the automobile industry, have committed themselves to a metric conversion, and all 50 states are committed to changing to the metric system in their educational systems. Great Britain has not completed its conversion after years of effort. Australia, on the other hand, developed a carefully detailed planning and scheduling program for converting their building industry to the metric system and virtually completed this conversion in less than 5 years. The Canadian M-Day is January 1, 1978, at which time the Canadian construction industry will work mainly in the SI system.

The modernized metric system will be called the "International System of Units" with the international abbreviation "SI." In the United States and Canada, this system will replace the English system of units (pound, foot, etc.), which is also called the U.S. Customary System (USCS) and which has been in common use in most architectural and engineering disciplines. The metric system is the only system that has ever approached worldwide acceptance, and one of the major reasons the United States and Canada are "going metric" is that most of the technical world has already adopted the SI system.

The system is based on a very logical and easily understood interrelationship among linear measures, weights, and cubic and volume measures—all based on decimal units. The system thereby dispenses with the many varieties and combinations of the USCS system and substitutes only three—the meter, the liter, and the kilogram. The SI system has a very rational base: everything is in multiples or divisions of 10, with decimals eliminating fractions entirely. As a result, simplicity is inherent in the SI system, and this will become more apparent and rewarding as it becomes familiar to the construction industry.

The transition period will not be without many frustrations, but in the end the architectural profession may find that it has not been severely affected by the changeover. Although the industries that produce the items used in construction will be greatly affected by the retooling, retraining, new cataloging, etc., that will be necessary, a successful nationwide program of dimensional coordination can result in a far more efficient use of resources in manufacturing and field assembly. The resulting changes will require a complete rewriting of textbooks, design manuals, trade catalogs, and other technical building data, and of building codes and standards. But if there were ever a time to reevaluate traditional practices and procedures and to eliminate problem areas in design and construction, this is it. The opportunity to make the changes long-lasting and beneficial must not be lost.

The ability to divide a foot by 2, 3, 4, 6, and 12 may be viewed by many as an advantage when compared with the metric decimal system, but architects, engineers, and their draftors are well aware of the frustrations encountered when adding, subtracting, multiplying, and dividing feet, inches, and fractions. The foot-inch system bears a relationship to human stature and incorporates a convenient method of identifying the increments of a foot; one can learn to "feel" this relationship in reading and determining dimensions and values. Architects, engineers, draftors, contractors, and construction personnel have developed the ability to estimate dimensions and quantities of building components by visualizing their sizes and the spaces they occupy. Now all the key recognition factors will be changed, and the learning process will need to start all over again. The 2-ft 6-in door width and the 8-ft-high ceiling are well known and have easily identifiable characteristics, while the corresponding 762 mm and the 2.438 m express quite impersonal units. Even if these metrics were rounded off, the values would still be difficult to remember.

Probably the forming of a mental image of this new dimensional environment will be easier to achieve than the understanding of the relationship between the units, which are a combination of a number of units, such as those for power, heat values, pressure, and force. Although these combinations have been given simple names, learning these newer units may not help in applying them to design considerations. Recognition of the key relationship between the old and new values is important in the learning process; for example, recognizing that the 4-inch dimension is approximately equivalent to 100 mm, and 12 inches approximately equivalent to 300 mm, will establish a recognition factor for the whole range of dimensions, and, similarly, 100 000 Btu/hr and its approximate equivalent of 30 kW can become a fundamental recognition factor for heat values.

THE TRANSITION PERIOD

The U.S. building industry should promptly establish a target date for M-Day, on which construction with all metric-size products can begin. The experience of other countries dramatically illustrates that the shorter the transition period, the shorter the time that dual-size products will be a problem to the design and construction professions. Industry apparently realizes that the shorter the transition time, the less expensive the conversion process will be. The experience of others also has shown that a *soft conversion,* one in which existing dimensions are simply converted to their metric equivalents, is short-sighted and will eventually prove more expensive and certainly more confusing than a *hard conversion,* in which the sizes of nonconforming construction units are actually changed to dimensions that are even and workable metric numbers coordinated with the dimensions of other metric components.

The dimensional coordination of metrication will be difficult. In some cases, codes will determine the dimensional requirements, and as a result decisions on code changes must come first. In other cases, industry standards, such as the dimensions of framing lumber, will need to be made before code decisions can be made. And national agreements will have to be firmly established regarding the SI units to be used in construction and the principles to be applied to dimensional coordination before the revisions of standards and codes can be initiated. It is hoped that the design profession will be well represented on the decision-making bodies.

A caution to the reader is necessary. Until agreements can be better formalized between nations; until industry, standards associations, and codes committees can endorse standards of measure and size for the multitude of construction units; and until the design and construction professions can actually gain experience in working with the metric system, this transition period can be expected to produce changes in the SI units, methods of notations, and dimensional coordination. Amid this confusion of attitudes and conventions, this book, including this introduction to the metric system, is being produced; the author is presenting information which seems applicable at this time to a reasonable and coordinated method of applied metrication for the architectural design segment of the building construction industry. The author does not imply that the information and conventions contained herein have been formally adopted by nations or industry or the design profession, nor that they will be; only time will reveal what methods are chosen.

Once the agreements have been reached regarding metrication and its dimensional coordination, the design office will have the problem of putting it into use, and that will involve the training of the office personnel. In order to avoid duplication of effort, each office might delegate one individual or one group within the office to learn and then teach and consult with the other professionals within the office, especially in the preparation of the first drawings and contracts to use the SI units and metric procedures. Teaching/

learning aids should include (1) arranging metric markers horizontally and vertically on the drafting room wall, (2) posting conversion tables and conversion scales (Figure 5-8) at each work desk and drafting table, and (3) keeping readily available some metric-size objects, such as bricks, concrete blocks, and commonly used wood and metal sections for convenient measuring and visual association. Electronic calculators are already being developed to aid in making instant conversions.

METRIC UNITS TO BE USED

The system of metric measurement by SI units that the United States will be adopting is also being adopted by the other English-speaking nations (Great Britain, Canada, Australia, New Zealand, and South Africa), and differs from the metric system long in use in Europe and other parts of the world. Notable among the differences is the use of the newton as the SI unit of force, which separates mass and force; the older metric system uses the kilogram to indicate force *and* mass. Although the concept is changed, the result will produce little actual difference in the building-design values involved.

The foundation of the new system (as it will affect the building industry) lies in the six SI base units shown in Table 5-1.

TABLE 5-1   Base Units

Quantity	Unit	Symbol
Length	meter	m
Time	second	s
Mass	kilogram	kg
Electric current	ampere	A
Temperature	kelvin	K
Luminous intensity	candela	cd

TABLE 5-2 Derived Units (Named after Base Unit)

Quantity	Unit	Symbol
Area	square meter	m²
Volume	cubic meter	m³
Density	kilogram per cubic meter	kg/m³
Acceleration	meter per second squared	m/s²
Luminance	candela per square meter	cd/m²

TABLE 5-3 Derived Units (with Special Names)

Quantity	Unit	Symbol	Derivation
Force	newton	N	kg·m/s²
Work, energy	joule	J	N·m
Power	watt	W	J/s
Electric potential	volt	V	W/A
Illumination	lux	lx	lm/m²

The SI base units are combined to make new measurement units, which are referred to as *derived units*. These are of two kinds—those expressed in terms of the units from which they are derived and those given special names (see Tables 5-2 and 5-3).

In addition, there are a few *non-SI units* which may continue to be used along with the SI units (see Table 5-4).

Supplemental SI units, the radian and steradian, will be shown in some SI unit reference manuals, but these units will be little used in the construction industry, which will continue to use the familiar degree (°) and decimals of degrees based on 90° in a right angle.

The principal feature of the SI system is its decimal base. All

TABLE 5-4   Non-SI Units

Time	day, hour, and minute
Mass	metric ton, which equals 1000 kg (or approximately 2200 pounds)
Area	hectare, which equals 10 000 square meters (or approximately 2½ acres)
Volume	liter, which equals one-thousandth of a cubic meter (or approximately one quart)

multiples and submultiples of SI units are based on powers of 10 simply expressed by applying prefixes to the units, preferably using decimal multiples and submultiples which are related to the base unit by powers of 1000.

Notice that Table 5-5 does not include the centimeter. The order of magnitude between the centimeter and the millimeter is only 10, which increases the likelihood of error; it is incompatible in the drawing notation system, where it is unnecessary to add the unit symbol after each dimension when decimals of a meter are always carried to three places (such as 2.500) and millimeters are expressed in whole numbers (such as 2500).

The SI units will tend to reduce the number of measurement terms used in the building industry; the joule (J) will replace familiar units such as Btu, therm, and kilowatthour; and the watt (W) will replace horsepower, heat flow rate (Btu/h), refrigeration (tons), etc.

The unit of force is the newton (N), which is the force required to give a mass of one kilogram an acceleration of one meter per second per second ($1 m/s^2$). Mass is that nonchanging property of a body measured by comparing its weight with the weight of a known mass on a pair of scales measured in kilograms. Weight is a force proportional to the mass of a body and to the intensity of the

TABLE 5-5 Preferred Multiples and Submultiples

Prefix	Symbol	Factor	Magnitude
mega	M	10^6	1 000 000
kilo	k	10^3	1 000
milli	m	10^{-3}	0.001
micro	μ	10^{-6}	0.000 001

gravitational field. To better understand these relationships, consider a bale of cotton, the mass of which is measured in kilograms; the designer will describe the floor load for the cotton warehouse in densities of kilograms per square meter, and the structural engineer will use these load ratings in computing the stress determinations by changing the kilograms per square meter to newtons per square meter, or pascals (Pa).

For convenience of reference, Conversion Tables 5-11 through 5-14 and Figure 5-8 are included at the end of this chapter. These tables are intended to cover only those basic conversions that have frequent application to architectural design and drawing. Architects, engineers, and draftors will require more complete tables for technical use.

NOTATIONS OF THE SI UNITS

Notations of the SI units will be necessary on the drawings, in the specifications, and in letters and other typewritten or printed material. All of these documents will be used and interpreted by many persons in various geographic locations. Therefore, expressing units in a conventional manner that can be understood throughout the building construction industry is imperative.

The notations of the SI units appearing in legal documents, land descriptions, and in most letters will need to be very specific, with no chance of ambiguity. These documents are generally produced by typewriting or printing, and therefore the appending of the appropriate symbol after each measurement is not particularly time-consuming. However, architectural drawings are likely to be read by individuals reasonably familiar with the type of construction the drawings illustrate, and since drawings are generally produced by hand, it is logical and time-saving in the production process to eliminate every unnecessary symbol. For example, if the notation 250 can be understood to mean 250 m, the elimination of the "m" after each of a multitude of dimensions can prove extremely time-saving. Specifications are somewhat of a hybrid, produced by typewriting but written by architects and engineers to be read by the same persons who will read the corresponding drawings. Thus, the specifications may also include the more abbreviated notations system used on the drawings.

Under these circumstances the following general system of notations of the SI units is suggested:

Thousand Markers

1. No thousand marker need be used when only four digits are shown.
   4300

2. In numbers with many digits, legibility is improved by providing a space (never a comma) at every thousand point.
   1 230 000
   11 200

Decimal Points

1. The British prefer the decimal point to be raised, that is, to appear opposite the middle of the figure when printed or handwritten.
   0·2
   9·602

This poses no particular problem for hand lettering. However, the typewriter does not contain a special character above the line, and for uniformity in both hand lettering and typing (specifications and correspondence as well will be typed and will use SI units with decimals), it seems preferable to keep the decimal on the line in all instances.

　　0.2
　　9.602

2. With any expression less than unity, the decimal should be preceded by a zero.

　　0.1
　　0.02
　　0.0379

3. Whole numbers should be expressed without a decimal.

　　　2
　　300
　　3800 or 3 800

Writing the SI Symbols

1. Leave a single space between numerical value and symbol.
　　225 mm (not 225mm)

2. Express the symbol as if it were singular.
　　208 m (not 208 ms)

3. Use uppercase and lowercase letters appropriately.
　　kg kW (not Kg kw)

4. Write out "metric ton." The symbol "t" may be mistaken to stand for the USCS ton.

5. Observe that when symbols are raised to various powers, it is the *symbol* which is involved and not the attached number.
　　3 m^3 means $3(\text{m})^3$, not $3 \text{ m} \times 3 \text{ m} \times 3 \text{ m}$.
　　3 m^3 means 3 cubic meters, not 27 cubic meters.

6. Use a sloping line to separate numerator from denominator.
　　4 kg/m^2 (four kilograms per square meter)

7. Do not hyphenate a unit (use "millimeters", not "milli-meters"), and avoid hyphenating a unit at the end of a line (example: "milligram", not "milli-" on one line and "gram" on the next).

8. Use symbols denoting the same multiples or submultiples of the SI unit in expressing dimensional sizes. Do not mix different units.

    1200 × 625 mm
    or 1.200 × 0.625 m
    never 1.200 m × 625 mm

    In this manner, where figures are of the same multiples or submultiples and are separated by a multiplication sign, the metric symbol need only be given after the last figure.

9. Write dimensions to three places of decimals when meters involve decimals, thereby assuring visual compatibility with the same dimension when it is expressed in millimeters.

    7.612 m = 7612 mm
    0.150 m = 150 mm

Further Simplification for Drawings

1. When both meters and millimeters are used on drawings, it will be less confusing if the dimension is written to three decimal places—for example, 1.250. No unit symbol need be shown except when fewer decimal places are used, such as 1.25 m.

2. When no ambiguity can arise, symbols may be omitted according to these three rules (and these rules should be noted on the drawings):
    a. Whole numbers indicate millimeters.
    b. Numbers expressed to three decimal places indicate meters.
    c. All other dimensions must be followed by the unit symbol.

3. In the past there has been no general misunderstanding that lumber noted 2 × 4 × 10-0 described a member with nominal 2 × 4″ cross section and 10′-0″ length, or that plywood noted ½ × 4-0 × 8-0 described a panel ½″ thick × 4′-0″ wide × 8′-0″ long. Likewise there should be no ambiguity in interpreting the metric sizes when the SI units are *expressed in this sequence*—from least to greatest dimension (usually thickness, least width of face, then length) in accordance with these examples:

Unit	Dimensions
Door	900 × 2150
Ceiling panels	600 × 1200

Where one of the normal sequence dimensions (such as the thickness of doors or ceiling panels) might be specified, scheduled, or otherwise noted, conveniently eliminate that dimension from further drawing notations—for example, they might thereafter be listed:

Unit	Dimensional Sequence
Concrete block	100 × 200 × 400
Modular brick	100 × 67 × 200
Lumber	40 × 90 × 3.000
Wood boards	20 × 90 × 4.000
Ceiling panels	15 × 600 × 1200
Plywood panels	20 × 1200 × 2400
Gypsum drywall panels	15 × 1200 × 2400
Door	45 × 900 × 2150
Window	900 × 1500

Where one or more of the normal sequence dimensions is highly variable and would normally not be included in the drawing notes (such as cutting lengths of lumber or cutting panel sizes of gypsum drywall), the dimensions may be shortened to include only the dimension(s) of importance; for example:

Unit	Dimension(s)
Gypsum drywall	15
Studs	40 × 90
Plywood subfloor	20

For bolts and rods, the diameter should be stated first, followed by the length.

    13 × 300 (bolt)

If written in any other sequence, each size must be followed by the SI identification symbol.

4. When any ambiguity in the notation method is likely, an appropriate explanation note should be conspicuously placed on the drawings.

During the transition period, some products will appear in metric measure while others are still being produced with USCS measurements. When the design is based on a USCS product, the dimension should be followed by the metric conversion equivalent in parentheses; for example: 4″ (102). Conversely, when the design is based on a metric product, the dimension should be followed by the USCS equivalent in parentheses; for example: 200 (7⅞″).

DIMENSIONAL COORDINATION

The acceptance of metrication by the building industry and its eventual success will depend principally upon a simple and logical system of dimensional coordination. Consider the 4 × 8′ panel of plywood or gypsum board, with which all are familiar. The confusion is apparent when the size is translated to the exact metric equivalents of 1219.2 × 2438.4 mm. The mental image would be clearer and the figures would be easier to remember if they were rounded off to even numbers, such as 1200 × 2400 mm. But if the panels were made in this new size, they would not fit with other building components unless those components were dimensionally compatible. The concept of rounding off the figures is not a panacea, because rounding off to the nearest modular unit can result in a significant dimensional change; for example, the approximate difference at 4″ is ¹⁄₁₆″ or 1.6 mm, at 1′ it is ³⁄₁₆″ or 4.8 mm, and at 8′ it is nearly 1½″ or 38 mm.

What is needed, then, is a system of measurement for building components based on a simple unit, or module, which has multiples that fit compatibly with most building conditions. Canada has adopted the 100 mm module, and their metric dimension system is based on using multiples of this module, such as 1200 × 2400 mm for panel components. The concept of the 100 mm module has been widely suggested for the United States and presumably will be adopted. There is apparently no other basic module that can serve as well.

This module concept does not mean that every building component must exactly measure some multiple of this unit, for those components that are laid in coursing, such as the brick or the concrete block, must take into account the joint. Therefore the module may need to work with the center to center of joints or from the bed joint to the bed joint of units. This concept is not unlike that of the module system of the 4″ cube that has dominated American industry for many years. Many varieties of building components are multiples of this 4″ module, such as the 8 × 16″ concrete block, the 2 × 4′ ceiling panel, and the 4 × 8′ plywood panel. Only the last of these examples is an exact multiple size of the original 4″ unit; the block and the ceiling panel are of a lesser dimension to account for the jointing system, yet all components work to the module or grid. The same concept can be applied to the 100 mm module.

Although any increment of 100 mm will be possible, using multi-modules in the following frequencies will permit ease of association, and will likely be preferred in practice:

Horizontally: 300, 600, 900, 1200, 1500, 3000, and 6000 mm

Vertically (where smaller increments will be often necessary): 300 and 600 mm with increments of 100 mm up to 3000 mm

50 and 25 mm submodules for thin sections

For dimensions smaller than 25 mm, the submodules need further incrementation, and during the transition period, associating millimeters with fractions of an inch will be necessary. Associating 5 mm with 3/16 inch (nearly) will make for easy recognition and a logical transition to the 5 mm submodule (Table 5-6).

However, for some components the dimension may require an exact conversion, and the rounding off to the nearest 5 mm will not be acceptable.

The key building component of this entire modular metric system is the concrete block, for the multiples of its coursing will determine the compatible size of bricks, doors and doorframes, windows, and

TABLE 5-6   Submodules,
25 mm and Smaller

Fraction of Inch	Millimeters
3/16	5
3/8	10
9/16	15
3/4	20
1	25

many other items. Figure 5-1 illustrates the suggested modular sizes of concrete blocks and bricks and demonstrates the concept of coursing to an even modular dimension by using a uniform 10 mm joint. For the drawings, typical size notations for these modular units should read 100 × 200 × 400 for the block and 100 × 67 × 200 for the brick.

The standard 6'-8" and 7'-0" door heights have never been compatible with the block wall components, and they would remain a problem if used with the metric module system. Therefore, since any compatibility will require changes in door and frame sizes, Figure 5-2a illustrates a proposed logic for a new door height standard of 2150 mm. The 2150 mm height is approximately 7'-1", and would eliminate the 6'-8", 7'-0", and 7'-2" standards. Another standard height of 2350 mm (see Figure 5-2b) is envisioned. It would work well with the metal frame set at or near the ceiling heights suggested in Figure 5-4. New thickness standards for doors may emerge, or this may evolve into one common thickness. In the meantime, 35 and 45 mm closely approximate the present 1⅜" and 1¾" thicknesses, respectively.

If there should be any continued demand for a shorter standard door for residences and apartments, it should be 2050 mm in height (approximately 6'-9"). Although the top of a metal frame for

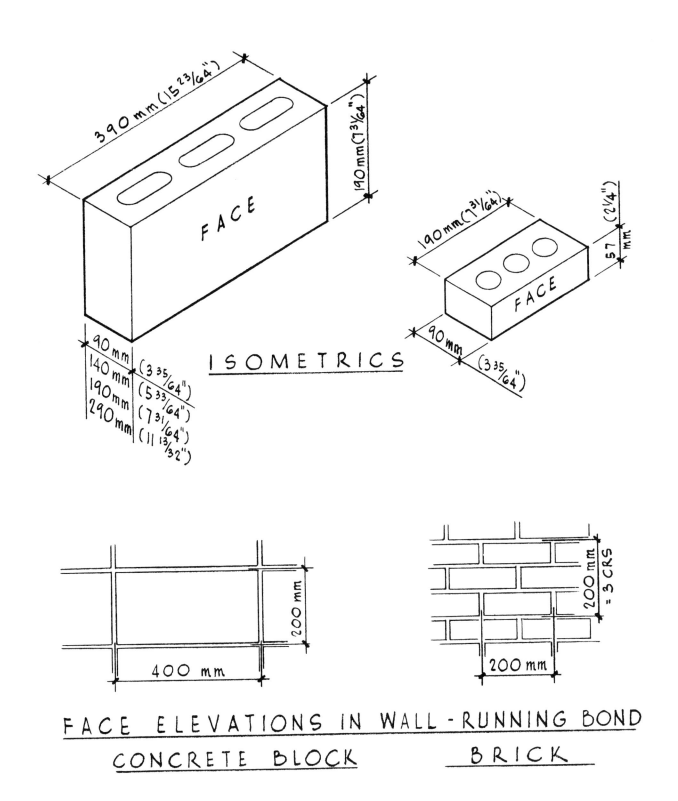

390 mm (15 23/64")
190 mm (7 3/64")
90 mm
140 mm (3 35/64")
190 mm (5 33/64")
290 mm (7 31/64")
(11 13/32")

FACE

ISOMETRICS

190 mm (7 31/64")
57 mm (2 1/4")
90 mm (3 35/64")

FACE

200 mm
400 mm

200 mm = 3 CRS
200 mm

FACE ELEVATIONS IN WALL - RUNNING BOND
CONCRETE BLOCK   BRICK

FIGURE 5-1 METRIC MODULAR MASONRY UNITS.

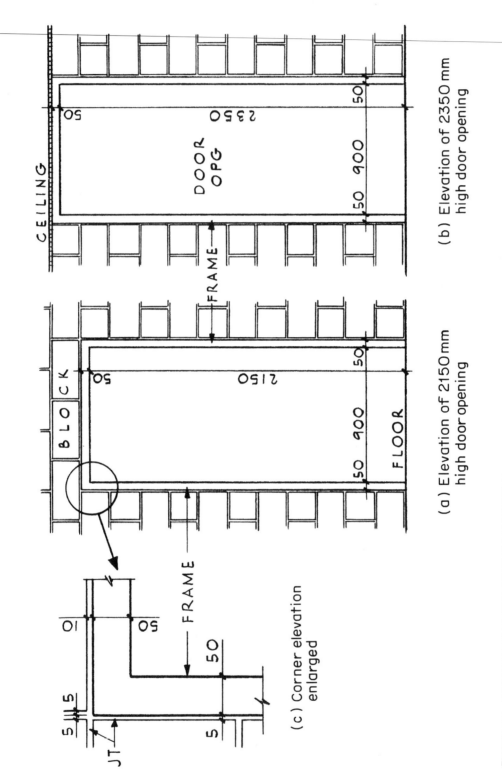

(a) Elevation of 2150 mm high door opening

(b) Elevation of 2350 mm high door opening

(c) Corner elevation enlarged

FIGURE 5-2 METRIC STEEL DOORFRAMES IN A BLOCK WALL.

this door would be at the midpoint of the normal block coursing, a filler-head unit of 4" (100 mm) high block would enable the frame to work favorably with the coursing. Since the majority of these 2050 mm height doors could be expected to be used in wood- and metal-frame construction, it would not be so critical for them to be compatible with the modular block.

Figure 5-3 details the fitting of the metal doorframe at the head

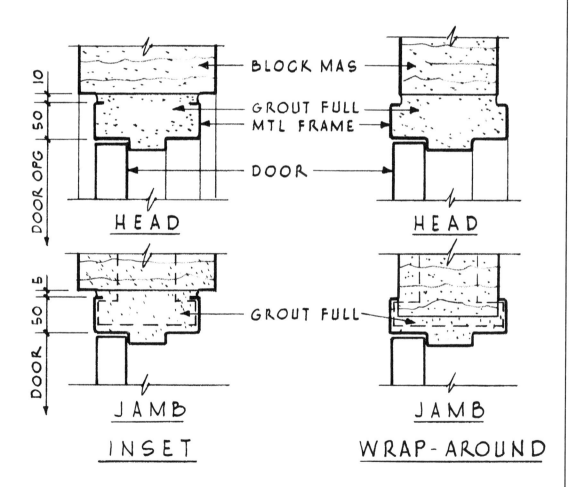

FIGURE 5-3   METRIC STEEL DOORFRAME INSTALLATIONS.

and jamb compatibly with the metric modular block dimensioning. This allows the retention of the current 2″ face frame dimension which would be called 50 mm—the outside of the frame occurring on the module line and thus allowing a 5 mm joint. This makes a fully compatible detail for a 2200 or 2400 mm-high frame that is set in the block opening, and when a wraparound condition is needed the jamb blocks can be fitted (and cut when necessary) into the jamb frame, and the lintel can be fitted over the grouted head rather than fitting the lintel blocks into the frame. The suggested new door and frame sizes are presented in Table 5-7.

The industry-proposed 1200 × 2400 mm wall-panel size, for such materials as gypsum drywall and plywood, will require basic changes in the traditional framing dimensions, such as the ceiling

TABLE 5-7   Door and Frame Sizes

Door Width Module		Doorframe Module	
Millimeters	Foot/Inch Equivalent	Millimeters	Foot/Inch Equivalent
600	2-0	700	2-4
700	2-4	800	2-8
800	2-8	900	3-0
900	3-0	1000	3-4
1100	3-8	1200	4-0

Door Height Module		Doorframe Module	
Millimeters	Foot/Inch Equivalent	Millimeters	Foot/Inch Equivalent
2050*	6-9	2100*	6-11
2150	7-1	2200	7-3
2350	7-9½	2400	7-10½

*Not a preferred size.

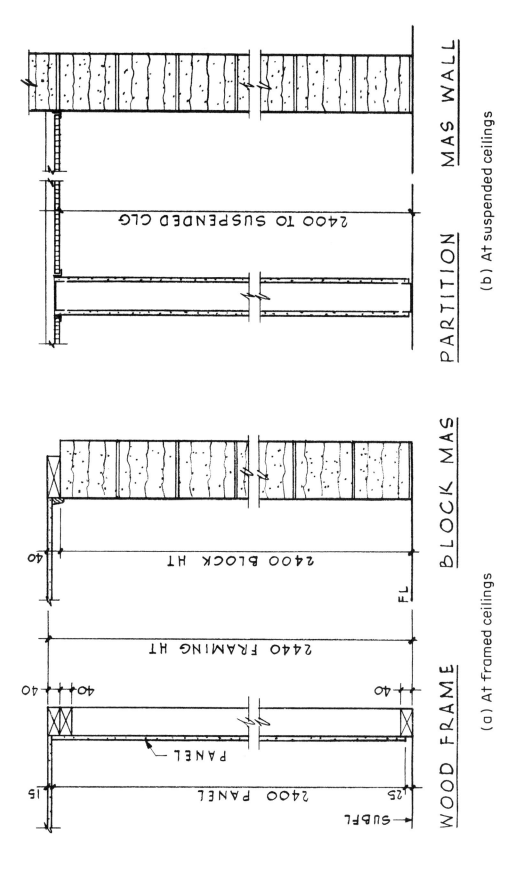

WOOD FRAME   BLOCK MAS

(a) At framed ceilings

PARTITION   MAS WALL

(b) At suspended ceilings

FIGURE 5-4   METRIC REPLACEMENT OF THE TRADITIONAL 8-FOOT CEILING HEIGHT.

height and the spacing of framing members. Figures 5-4a and 5-4b illustrate the one-story framing of both a wood stud wall and a modular block wall that would be compatible with the new panel dimension, and the corresponding spacing of stud and joist framing would be either 400 or 600 mm on centers in lieu of 16″ or 24″. These vertical sections show a ceiling-frame height of 2440 mm which, with a ceiling thickness of 15 mm, leaves a clear height of 2425 mm, or approximately 7′-11½″. For wood framing, the 2400 mm wall panel below a 15 mm thick ceiling panel leaves 25 mm at the panel base for working the panel up into place and yet allows sufficient overlap to nail the panel to the sole plate. The length of precut wood studs would be 2320 mm.

In the case of buildings with block masonry walls and partitions of block masonry or gypsum drywall (framed with either metal or wood), the suspended ceiling may be placed at 2400 mm off the floor, as in Figure 5-4c, thereby working to the advantage of all these assemblies and coordinating with the top of the 2400 mm doorframe (2350 mm door).

The convenient notation of panel thicknesses for plywood and other wallboards should be in increments of 5 mm (10, 15, 20, and 25 mm). (Refer to Table 5-6.) However, if industry makes a soft conversion corresponding to ⅜″, ½″, ⅝″, and ¾″, more confusing increments may evolve.

Framing lumber has seldom been furnished in actual dimension; for example, the 2 × 4 may be near full size when furnished rough-cut and green. When surfaced-four-sides the dimensions will approximate 1⅝″ × 3⅝″ green or 1½″ × 3½″ dry. Therefore, the nominal, or modular, dimension has usually been used in floor-plan dimensioning (for partition thicknesses, etc.) and the actual dimension in large-scale detailing. A similar dimension coordination is suggested in Table 5-8, with nominal dimensions rounded out to the nearest workable figures, since the softwood industry will probably make a relatively soft conversion.

The nearest substitute for the 2″ × 6″ × 16′-0″ would, therefore,

TABLE 5-8 Softwood Lumber and
Board Sizes

Cross Section		Length	
Inches (dry)	Nominal Millimeters Equivalent	Meters	Nearest Feet
3/8	10	1.200	4.0
9/16	15	1.800	6.0
3/4	20	2.400	8.0
1	25	3.000	10.0
1½	40	3.600	12.0
3½	90	4.200	14.0
5½	140	4.800	16.0
7¼	190	5.400	18.0
9¼	240	6.000	20.0
11¼	290	7.200	24.0

be 40 mm × 140 mm × 4.8 m (approximately 1½″ × 5½″ × 15′-9″), and would be written as 40 × 140 × 4.800 on the drawing (or 40 × 140 when lengths are not specified). This suggested method avoids grossly inaccurate cross-section dimensions (for example, the former nominal 2″ is ½″ larger than the actual 1½″, or a difference of 12.7 mm) and employs the nearest logical metric dimension. This provides rational, *nearly exact* dimensions for drawing detailing and noting.

Table 5-9 describes the probable popular sizes of concrete reinforcing bars. Lengths would be expressed to the nearest 5 mm with a standard length of 12 m.

The foregoing sizes of probable or suggested building components form the basic structure of the proposed dimension coordina-

TABLE 5-9 Reinforcing Bar Sizes

Size (dia.), mm	Area, mm²	Weight, kg/m	Approx. Size, in
6	28	0.222	¼
10	79	0.617	⅜
12	113	0.888	½
16	201	1.580	⅝
20	314	2.470	¾
25	491	3.860	1
32	804	6.310	1¼

TABLE 5-10 Drawing Scales to Use

Metric Scale	Nearest Comparable Foot-Inch Scale	Use for
1:500 (2 mm to 1 m)	1″ = 40′	Site plans
1:200 (5 mm to 1 m)	¹⁄₁₆″ = 1′	
1:200 (5 mm to 1 m)	¹⁄₁₆″ = 1′	Floor plans
1:100 (10 mm to 1 m)	⅛″ = 1′	
1:50 (20 mm to 1 m)	¼″ = 1′	
1:20 (50 mm to 1 m)	½″ = 1′	Details
1:10 (100 mm to 1 m)	1″ = 1′	
1:5 (200 mm to 1 m)	3″ = 1′	
1:1 (full size)	Full size	

tion system. Forthcoming handbooks, catalogs, and other technical data prepared by industry will set the actual dimensional standards for their respective products, such as structural steel, steel reinforcing bars, steel sheet and strip, pipe, and tubing, and for manufactured components such as cabinets and household appliances.

DRAWING SCALES

The drawing scales for various types of drawings are suggested in Table 5-10. The scale should be stated on every drawing, and a graphic scale should be included for those drawings that will be reproduced at a reduced size.

TYPICAL DRAWING DIMENSIONING

Figures 5-5 and 5-6 illustrate a floor plan and a doorframe section that convey some of the principles of metric dimensioning.

SITE PLANS

Most sites on which buildings are planned can be contoured in 1 m intervals, with 0.5 m intervals where grades change abruptly or where the terrain is particularly flat. Spot grades for bench marks and precise elevations, as well as horizontal dimensions, should be given in meters to three places of decimals or as the accuracy requires. The meter identification "m" may be eliminated by placing a note on the drawings to the effect that "site dimensions are given in meters."

In order to avoid the minus sign, which can be easily misread, a datum or fixed reference point (temporary bench mark) may be established to the effect that all other levels will be positive. This datum should be indicated clearly on the drawings, and all other related grades and elevations should be expressed in meters to three places of decimal, as in Figure 5-7. Wherever sea-level elevation is available, the datum should be related to sea level in order to better coordinate with terrain maps and with sewers and other elements which are usually related to sea level.

DRAWING SHEET SIZES

Probably the most popular drawing paper size has been the 24 × 36" sheet, with 30 × 42" used for larger drawings and 18 × 24" and

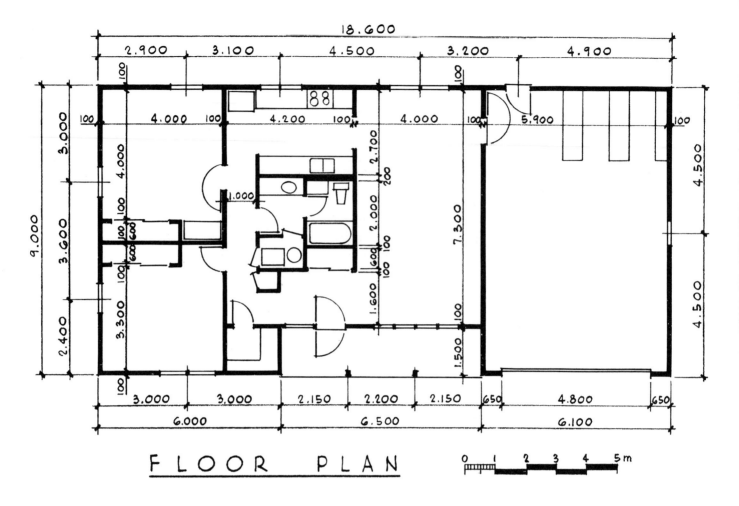

FIGURE 5-5 FLOOR PLAN WITH METRIC DIMENSIONS.

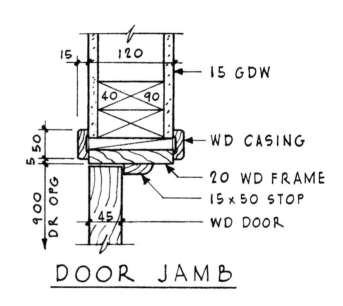

DOOR JAMB

FIGURE 5-6 DOORFRAME SECTION WITH METRIC DIMENSIONS.

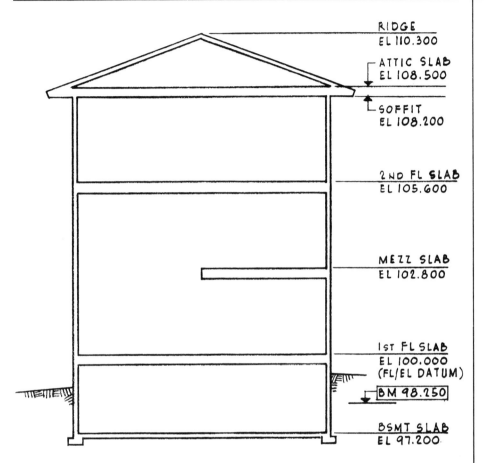

RIDGE
EL 110.300

ATTIC SLAB
EL 108.500

SOFFIT
EL 108.200

2ND FL SLAB
EL 105.600

MEZZ SLAB
EL 102.800

1ST FL SLAB
EL 100.000
(FL/EL DATUM)

BM 98.250

BSMT SLAB
EL 97.200

FIGURE 5-7 FLOOR ELEVATIONS AND DATUM FOR A VERTICAL BUILDING SECTION.

8½ × 11″ used for smaller ones. The probable basic metric size for architectural drawings will be 594 × 841 mm (approximately 23⅜″ × 33⅛″), which may then be cut or folded to smaller dimensions of 594 × 420 mm, 297 × 420 mm, 210 × 297 mm, 148 × 210 mm, and 105 × 148 mm. A 600 × 900 mm size would be simpler.

REFERENCE TABLES AND FIGURES

Figure 5-8 and Tables 5-11 through 5-14 are shown here for general reference in establishing dimensions and in making conversions.

118

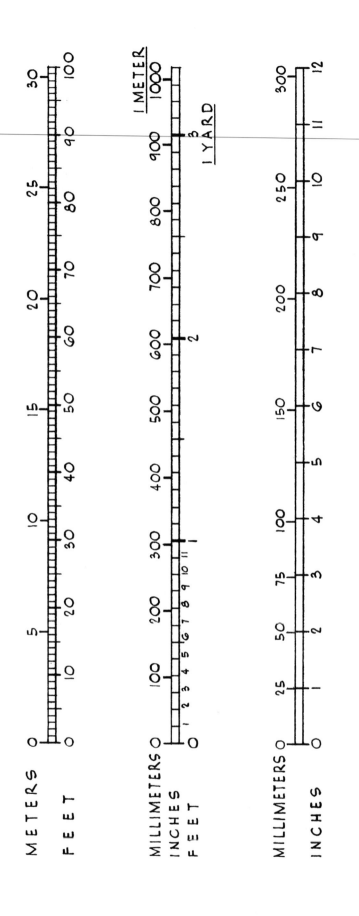

FIGURE 5-8 METRIC EQUIVALENT SCALES.

TABLE 5-11 Conversion: Fractions of an Inch to Millimeters (¹⁄₃₂″ through 1″)

Inch	mm	Inch	mm	Inch	mm	Inch	mm
1/32	0.8	9/32	7.1	17/32	13.5	25/32	19.8
1/16	1.6	5/16	7.9	9/16	14.3	13/16	20.6
3/32	2.4	11/32	8.7	19/32	15.1	27/32	21.4
1/8	3.2	3/8	9.5	5/8	15.9	7/8	22.2
5/32	4.0	11/32	10.3	21/32	16.7	29/32	23.0
3/16	4.8	7/16	11.1	11/16	17.5	15/16	23.8
7/32	5.6	15/32	11.9	23/32	18.3	31/32	24.6
1/4	6.4	1/2	12.7	3/4	19.1	1	25.4

TABLE 5-12 Conversions: Feet and Inches to Meters (1″ through 10′)

Feet \ Inches	0	1	2	3	4	5	6	7	8	9	10	11
0		0.025	0.051	0.076	0.102	0.127	0.152	0.178	0.203	0.229	0.254	0.279
1	0.305	0.330	0.356	0.381	0.406	0.432	0.457	0.483	0.508	0.533	0.559	0.584
2	0.610	0.635	0.660	0.686	0.711	0.737	0.762	0.787	0.813	0.838	0.864	0.889
3	0.914	0.940	0.965	0.991	1.016	1.041	1.067	1.092	1.118	1.143	1.168	1.194
4	1.219	1.245	1.270	1.295	1.321	1.346	1.372	1.397	1.422	1.448	1.473	1.499
5	1.524	1.549	1.575	1.600	1.626	1.651	1.676	1.702	1.727	1.753	1.778	1.803
6	1.829	1.854	1.880	1.905	1.930	1.956	1.981	2.007	2.032	2.057	2.083	2.108
7	2.134	2.159	2.184	2.210	2.235	2.261	2.286	2.311	2.337	2.362	2.388	2.413
8	2.438	2.464	2.489	2.515	2.540	2.565	2.591	2.616	2.642	2.667	2.692	2.718
9	2.743	2.769	2.794	2.819	2.845	2.870	2.896	2.921	2.946	2.972	2.997	3.023
10	3.048											

TABLE 5-13 Conversions: Feet to Meters (1′ through 100′)

Feet	Meters	Feet	Meters	Feet	Meters	Feet	Meters	Feet	Meters
1	0.305	21	6.401	41	12.497	61	18.593	81	24.689
2	0.610	22	6.706	42	12.802	62	18.898	82	24.994
3	0.914	23	7.010	43	13.106	63	19.202	83	25.298
4	1.219	24	7.315	44	13.411	64	19.507	84	25.603
5	1.524	25	7.620	45	13.716	65	19.812	85	25.908
6	1.829	26	7.925	46	14.021	66	20.117	86	26.213
7	2.134	27	8.230	47	14.316	67	20.422	87	26.518
8	2.438	28	8.534	48	14.630	68	20.726	88	26.822
9	2.743	29	8.839	49	14.935	69	21.031	89	27.127
10	3.048	30	9.144	50	15.240	70	21.336	90	27.432
11	3.353	31	9.449	51	15.545	71	21.641	91	27.737
12	3.658	32	9.754	52	15.850	72	21.946	92	28.042
13	3.962	33	10.058	53	16.154	73	22.250	93	28.346
14	4.267	34	10.363	54	16.459	74	22.555	94	28.651
15	4.572	35	10.668	55	16.764	75	22.860	95	28.956
16	4.877	36	10.973	56	17.069	76	23.165	96	29.261
17	5.182	37	11.278	57	17.374	77	23.470	97	29.566
18	5.486	38	11.582	58	17.678	78	23.774	98	29.870
19	5.791	39	11.887	59	17.983	79	24.079	99	30.175
20	6.096	40	12.192	60	18.288	80	24.384	100	30.480

TABLE 5-14   Metric Conversions: Imperial to SI Units

Measurement	Imperial Unit	SI Unit	Symbol	Conversion Equivalent
Length	mile	kilometer	km	1 mi = 1.609 km
	yard	meter	m	1 yd = 0.9144 m
	foot	meter	m	1 ft = 0.3048 m
		millimeter	mm	= 304.8 mm
	inch	millimeter	mm	1 in = 25.40 mm
Area	square mile	square kilometer	km²	1 mi² = 2.590 km²
		hectare	ha	= 259.0 ha
	acre	hectare	ha	1 acre = 0.4047 ha
		square meter	m²	= 4046.9 m²
	square yard	square meter	m²	1 yd² = 0.8361 m²
	square foot	square meter	m²	1 ft² = 0.0929 m²
	square inch	square millimeter	mm²	1 in² = 645.2 mm²
Volume	cubic yard	cubic meter	m³	1 yd³ = 0.7646 m³
	cubic foot	cubic meter	m³	1 ft³ = 0.02832 m³
		liter	L	= 28.32 L
	cubic inch	cubic millimeter	mm³	1 in³ = 16390 mm³
		milliliter	mL	= 16.39 mL
		liter	L	= 0.01639 L
Mass	short ton (2000 lb)	kilogram	kg	1 short ton = 907.185 kg
	kip (1000 lb)	kilogram	kg	1 kip = 453.59 kg
	pound	kilogram	kg	1 lb = 0.4536 kg
	ounce	gram	g	1 oz = 28.35 g
Mass per Unit Area	pound per square foot	kilogram per square meter	kg/m²	1 lb/ft² = 4.882 kg/m²
	pound per square inch	kilogram per square meter	kg/m²	1 lb/in² = 703.07 kg/m²
	ounce per square foot	gram per square meter	g/m²	1 oz/ft² = 305.15 g/m²
Density	pound per cubic foot	kilogram per cubic meter	kg/m³	1 lb/ft³ = 16.02 kg/m³
	pound per cubic inch	gram per cubic centimeter	g/cm³	1 lb/in³ = 27.68 g/cm³
		megagram per cubic meter	Mg/m³	= 27.68 Mg/m³
Force (Structural)	pounds force	newton	N	1 lbf = 4.448 N
	pound force per foot	newton per meter	N/m	1 lbf/ft = 14.59 N/m
	pound force per inch	newton per millimeter	N/mm	1 lbf/in = 0.1751 N/mm
	kip force (1000 lbf)	kilonewton	kN	1 kipf = 4.448 kN
Bending Moment	pounds force foot	newton meter	N·m	1 lbf·ft = 1.356 N·m
	pounds force inch	newton meter	N·m	1 lbf·in = 0.1130 N·m
		newton millimeter	N·mm	= 113.0 N·mm
	kip force inch	newton meter	N·m	1 kipf·in = 113.0 N·m

Measurement	Imperial Unit	SI Unit	Symbol	Conversion Equivalent
Section Modulus	inch³	millimeter³	mm³	1 in³ = 16 390 mm³
Capacity	quart (U.S.)	milliliter	mL	1 qt = 946.353 mL
	pint (U.S.)	milliliter	mL	1 pt = 473.177 mL
	fluid ounce (U.S.)	milliliter	mL	1 fl oz = 29.574 mL
Volume Rate of Flow	cubic feet per minute	liter per second	L/s	1 ft³/min = 0.4719 L/s
	cubic feet per second	cubic meter per second	m³/s	1 ft³/sec = 0.02832 m³/s
	cubic inch per second	milliliter per second	mL/s	1 in³/sec = 16.39 mL/s
	U.S. gallon per hour	milliliter per second	mL/s	1 gal/hr = 1.05150 mL/s
	U.S. gallon per minute	liter per second	L/s	1 gal/min = 0.063090 L/s
Fuel Capacity	U.S. gallon per mile	liter per kilometer	L/km	1 gal/min = 2.352 L/km
	miles per gallon (U.S.)	kilometers per liter	km/L	1 mi/gal = 0.425 km/L
Velocity	miles per hour	kilometer per hour	km/h	1 mi/h = 1.609 km/h
	feet per minute	meter per minute	m/min	1 ft/min = 0.3048 m/min
	feet per second	meter per second	m/s	1 ft/s = 0.3048 m/s
	inch per second	millimeter per second	mm/s	1 in/sec = 25.4 mm/s
Temperature	°Fahrenheit	degree Celsius	°C	$t°C = 0.5556 (t°F-32)$
Temp. interval	°Fahrenheit	degree Celsius	°C	1°F = 0.5556°C
Heat	Btu	joule	J	1 Btu = 1055 J
		kilojoule	kJ	1 Btu = 1.055 kJ
Heat flow rate	Btu per hour	watt	W	1 Btu/h = 0.2931 W
		kilowatt	kW	1 Btu/h = 0.0002931 kW
Density of heat flow rate	Btu per square foot per hour	watt per square meter	W/m²	1 Btu/ft²·hr = 3.155 W/m²
Thermal conductivity (or K)	Btu inch per square foot per hour per °F	watt per meter per degree Celsius	W/m·°C	1 Btu·in/ft²·h·°F = 0.1442 W/m·°C
Thermal conductance (or U)	Btu per square foot per hour per degree Fahrenheit	watt per square meter per degree Celsius	W/m²·°C	1 Btu/ft²·h·°F = 5.678 W/m²·°C
Refrigeration	ton	watt	W	1 ton = 3519 W
Power	horsepower	watt	W	1 hp = 745.7 W
		kilowatt	kW	0.7457 kW
Lighting	footcandle (fc)	lux	lx	1 fc = 10.76 lx
	lumen per square foot	lux	lx	1 lm/ft² = 10.76 lx

METRIC BIBLIOGRAPHY

Hicks, Tyler G., *McGraw-Hill Metrication Manual,* McGraw-Hill Book Company, New York, 1972.

National Bureau of Standards, Technical Note 915, *Metrication Problems in the Construction Codes and Standards Sectors,* U.S. Government Printing Office, Washington, 1976.

Sliwa, Jon A., and Leslie Fairweather, *VNR Metric Handbook,* Van Nostrand Reinhold Company, New York, 1969.

6

DETAILING AND SCHEDULING

ORGANIZING AND CONTROLLING THE DETAILING

To ensure a balance between the quantity of drawings necessary for the specific project and the production-hour limit (see Chapter 1), the project captain should make a preliminary listing of all plans, elevations, details, schedules, and other information that is to appear on the drawings. Considerable thought must be given to this listing in order to eliminate unnecessary drawings and duplication in the drawings and yet ensure that every necessary drawing will be included. Adjustments to this preliminary listing will be necessary as the drawings develop.

Unless the details are a virtual carbon copy of a previous project, a great amount of time can be wasted by drawing the details directly on the finished tracing. Most detailing involves a considerable amount of trial-and-error and thus much erasing, for good detailing is a developmental process by which the drawing and the project are progressively improved. Therefore, a preliminary draft (or *control-detail*) should be made of all complicated details, drawing the outline of materials accurately to scale, without hatching, and writing (not lettering) the essential notes, as in Figure 6-1. The objective is to graphically describe the project essentials only in outline as accurately and as quickly as possible—the thought processes thereby keeping more closely aligned with the design concept and leaving the nitty-gritty aspects of sheet arrangement, line weights, hatching, and lettering until the detail is traced as a final drawing. When several are assigned to a project, efficiency favors the project captain or other well-experienced draftors preparing the control-details and the less experienced draftors making the final drawings.

Although the *control-detailing concept* may at first appear to be a duplication of the drawing effort, the production staff will find this a very efficient and time-saving process, and the benefits are as significant for only one person as they are for a team. Additional advantages of control-detailing are (1) that the bugs can be discovered before the final drawing is made, (2) that the accuracy is

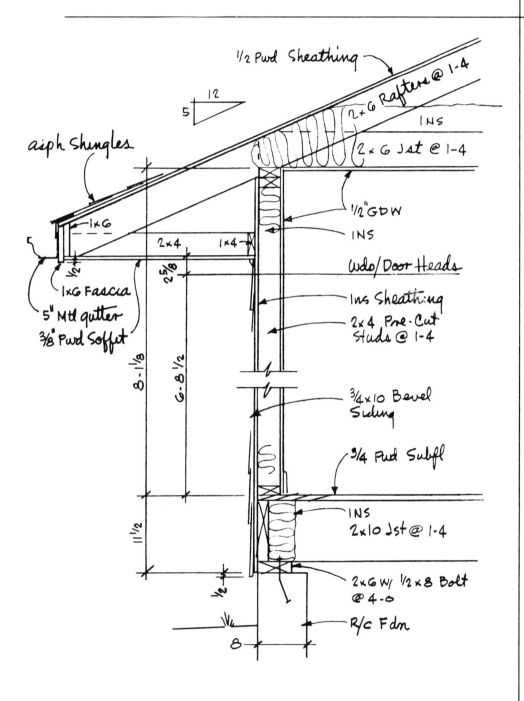

½ Pwd Sheathing

2+6 Rafters @ 1-4

INS

2 × 6 Jst @ 1-4

asph shingles

1×6

12
5

½

½"GDW

INS

2×4   1×4

Wdo/Door Heads

2⅝

1×6 Fascia
5" Mtl gutter
⅜ Pwd Soffit

Ins Sheathing

2×4 Pre-Cut
Studs @ 1-4

8-1⅛

6-8½

¾×10 Bevel
Siding

¾ Pwd Subfl

INS
2×10 Jst @ 1-4

11½

2×6 w/ ½×8 Bolt
@ 4-0

½

R/c Fdn

8

FIGURE 6-1   CONTROL-DETAIL OF A VERTICAL WALL SECTION.

improved for drawing and dimensioning, (3) that the physical size of many of the details is established prior to final sheet organization and spacing, and (4) that the need for additional details may be discovered before the final tracings are made.

A fundamental part of developing the construction essentials is the process of discovering, developing, and illustrating one detail and then another. A logical flow of that discovery and development is provided when drawing the details in the following sequence:

1. Small-scale longitudinal and cross sections of the building
2. Basic wall section(s)
3. Stair section(s)
4. Elevator section(s)
5. Vertical line diagram section for dimension control (see Figure 4-10)
6. Other sections establishing critical structural and space conditions

Once the control-details have been prepared and coordinated, the project architect should check them carefully. Changes are inevitable, and many of these changes may be quickly made by correction notes or supplemental freehand sketches, all of which can then be more accurately drawn and coordinated in the final tracings.

A point of caution! In this or any other drawing process, one of the greatest wastes of time results from the failure to record all the necessary dimensions and notes at the time they are first determined. For example, in the control-detailing process the draftor will be establishing critical features such as the dimensions of window openings, the elevation of the top of the steel joists, the coursing height of a masonry wall, the projection of an eave, and other essential decisions on materials, dimensions, and working points. These decisions must not be lost in the hurry to move from one detail to another. They must be recorded by notes and dimensions on the drawing as promptly as they are discovered and decided upon; otherwise the same thought processes will have to be repeated later.

SIMPLIFICATION OF DETAILS

Drawings are diagrammatic and need to be detailed only so far as to adequately illustrate the required construction. They should be simplified so that they include only the information necessary (and certainly no less information than necessary) for a complete communication from those preparing the drawings to those who will read them and build from them. Many details may be analyzed by these essentials:

Necessary	*Unnecessary*
Accurately drawn	Dimensions and identification adequately appearing elsewhere
Essential dimensions	
Identification of all materials by note or symbol	Notes repeated in the specifications
Details and instructions essential to the assembly and installation	Notes that can be more adequately described in the specifications
Anchorages not included in structural drawings	Excessive detailing of manufactured products
Special features at variance with standard construction	Repetition of structural, mechanical, or electrical detailing
Coordinated with structural, mechanical, and electrical details	Excessive hatching

Often very simplified diagrams can explain a situation as well as a complex detail or a lengthy note. An anchor bolt (½" diameter, 10" long, hooked 2″ at the lower end and with nut and washer at the wood plate) may be adequately illustrated, as in Figure 6-2*b*. In Figure 6-2*a* only the designation of the opening to receive the heating/cooling unit is essential; the unit need only be shown in outline, leaving any other related information for the manufacturer's shop drawings.

Windows are typically an assembly of many complex parts. The detailing of the parts may be important to the manufacturer's fabrications, but they are not of the same importance to the builder, whose primary need for the detail is to understand the installation requirements surrounding the window. Therefore, a section may be illustrated by a simplified line diagram as in Figure 6-3*a*, and the window occurring on the building elevations may be similarly simplified by eliminating superfluous lines, as in Figure 6-3*b*.

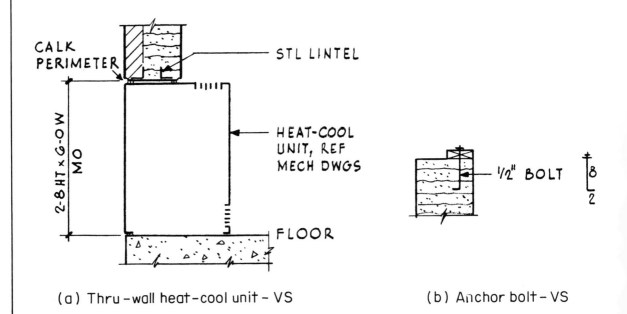

(a) Thru–wall heat–cool unit – VS   (b) Anchor bolt – VS

FIGURE 6-2 SIMPLIFICATION OF DETAILS.

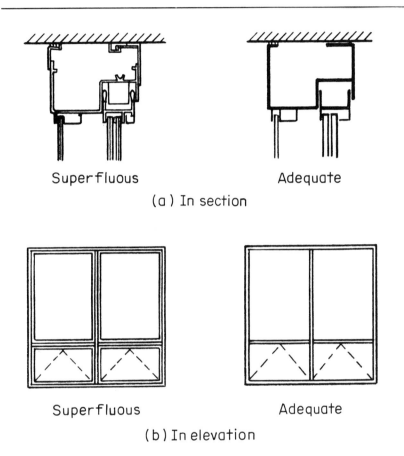

Superfluous   Adequate

(a) In section

Superfluous   Adequate

(b) In elevation

FIGURE 6-3 SIMPLIFIED WINDOW DIAGRAMS.

Drawing a series of very similar details is frequently necessary to illustrate the important variations of the construction. Since it seems natural to draw and to read details from left to right, the prime detail of the series (such as a basic wall section) may be drawn on the left, completely dimensioned and noted, as in Figure 6-4a. The other related details may then be drawn in a following pattern, as in Figure 6-4b, without repeating dimensions and notes that are included or reasonably implied in the prime detail.

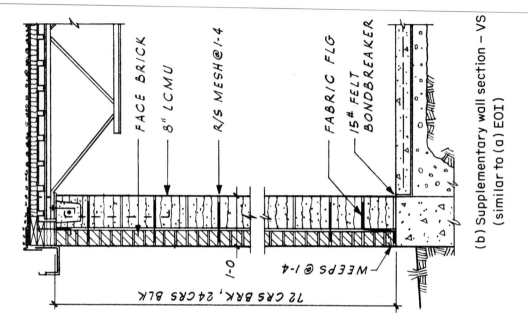

FACE BRICK
8" LCMU
R/S MESH @ 1-4

FABRIC FLG
15# FELT BONDBREAKER

WEEPS @ 1-4

12 CRS BRK, 24 CRS BLK

1-0

(b) Supplementary wall section – VS
(similar to (a) EOI)

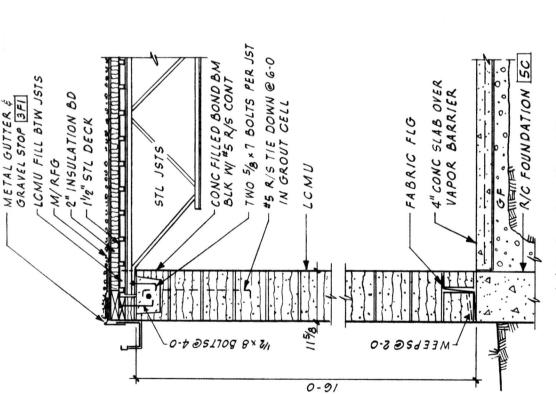

METAL GUTTER & GRAVEL STOP 3FI
LCMU FILL BTW JSTS
M/RFG
2" INSULATION BD
1½" STL DECK

STL JSTS

CONC FILLED BOND BM BLK W/ #5 R/S CONT
TWO ⅝ × 7 BOLTS PER JST
#5 R/S TIE DOWN @ 6-0 IN GROUT CELL
LCMU

FABRIC FLG
4" CONC SLAB OVER VAPOR BARRIER
GF
R/C FOUNDATION 5C

½ × 8 BOLTS @ 4-0

11⅝

WEEPS @ 2-0

16-0

(a) Basic wall section – VS

FIGURE 6-4 BASIC AND SUPPLEMENTARY WALL SECTIONS.

In residential and other buildings where the framing is relatively simple, the structural detailing may frequently be combined with the architectural detailing. In more complex buildings, the engineering drawings will illustrate the structural conditions in detail, and that amount of detail need not, and should not, be illustrated again in the related architectural drawings. The architectural drawings should include the structural elements in very simplified form. The concrete may be drawn in outline, eliminating reinforcement details, and the structural steel may be drawn very diagrammatically in outline. In similar fashion, the indications of mechanical and electrical equipment should be simplified on the architectural drawings, as in Figure 6-2*a*, leaving the further details to the mechanical-electrical engineering drawings and to the manufacturer's shop drawings.

Generally, floor plans are best illustrated by a complete hatching of walls and partitions, as in Figure 6-5*a*. However, the indication of

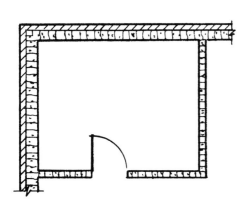

(a) Floor plan hatching of
walls and partitions

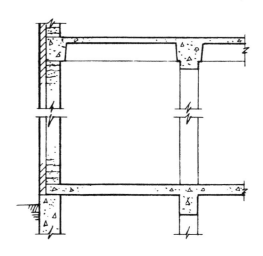

(b) Hatching in section – VS

FIGURE 6-5 HATCHING IN PLAN AND SECTION.

materials in sectioned details may be adequate when limited to a brief hatching at each change of direction, at breaks in construction, at ends of drawings, and at changes in materials, as in Figure 6-5b.

The symbol for *miscellaneous materials* is produced by a half-tone (usually colored) pencil poché on the back side of the tracing for normal reproduction processes. It is a quick method for simple identification of a large area or of a quantity of details of the same material, and is widely used as a substitute for the concrete symbol in making structural drawings. But since the use of this symbol is not limited to concrete, the material must be noted appropriately on the drawings.

Excessive hatching is time-consuming and unnecessary if the material is properly identified. In Figure 6-6, properly labeled plywood is obviously plywood, without excessive hatching.

Nearly everything must be hung from, supported by, or otherwise attached to another building component. The major items of structural attachments are normally engineered and detailed, but the myriad of supports and fastenings required for hanging cabinets, stabilizing partition heads, anchoring ledgers, attaching railings, wire suspensions, nailings, and other attachments are left to the architectural drawings; and too often these are left to the mechanics to solve in the field. Critical fastenings should be engineered. Every office should establish adequate and easy-to-use *tables for normal fastening conditions* of nails, screws, bolts, expansion anchors, wire hangings, railings, and other attachments to assist in

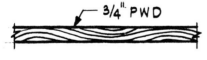

(a) Adequate hatching

(b) Superfluous hatching

FIGURE 6-6 SIMPLIFIED HATCHING.

selecting the correct fastenings; and these should be indicated in the details. The specifications may cover the more generalized and less critical fastenings.

APPROPRIATE SCALE

Even with many exceptions, drawings should generally be of adequate size when drawn to the following scales:

Site plan: 1″ = 20′; residences 1″ = 10′ preferred

Floor plans: ⅛″ = 1′-10″; residences and remodelings ¼″ = 1′-0″

Foundation plans: same scale as floor plans

Roof plans: same scale as floor plans, except they may be at reduced scale where uncomplicated

Exterior elevations: ⅛″ = 1′-0″; ¼″ = 1′-0″ for residences

Wall sections: ½″ = 1′-0″; 1½″ = 1′-0″ for enlarged details

Wall sections (residences): 1″ = 1′-0″

Stair sections: ⅜″ = 1′-0″; 1″ = 1′-0″ enlarged details

Foundation details: ½″ = 1′-0″

Building sections: ⅛″ = 1′-0″; ¼″ = 1′-0″ for residences or where some amount of detail is presented

Interior wall elevations: ⅛″ = 1′-0″

Door and window sections: 1½″ = 1′-0″; 3″ = 1′-0″ where more specifics are required

Reflected ceiling plans: same scale as floor plans, except they may be at reduced scale where uncomplicated

Cabinet elevations: ⅜″ = 1′-0″; ½″ = 1′-0″ where more specifics are required

Cabinet sections: ½″ = 1′-0″; ¾″ = 1′-0″ where more specifics are required; 1½″ or 3″ = 1′-0″ for enlarged details

Fireplace sections: ½″ = 1′-0″

Other details: Generally at the smallest scale that will be easy to draw and easy to read without crowding—and without wasting sheet space

When drawings will be reproduced at smaller size, the original may need to be drawn commensurately larger. However, readability at reduced scale may be more affected by the lettering size than by the line work (see Chapter 3).

COORDINATION WITH THE SPECIFICATIONS

The drawings and the specifications should be carefully coordinated to avoid duplication and conflict. The office policy must be conclusive as to what will appear in the drawings and what will be reserved for the specifications. The drawings should illustrate and dimension the construction and identify the materials; the specifications should then describe the quality of the materials and the specifics of the installations. For example, the identification of the metal gutter and gravel stop in Figure 6-4a will be supported (elsewhere in the drawings) by an enlarged detail with additional dimensions and specifics of the gutter profile, the supporting straps and their spacings, the attachments, etc. The specifications would then identify the gauge and type of metal and the further specifics of fabrication, assembly, and installation.

During the development of the drawings, decisions on the make, type, finishes, and other specifics of a material may have (and often should have) been made by the project architect or a draftor, but some of the decision making may be left to the specifications writer. For example, if the draftor has established the gauges or types of metal for the gutter and gravel stop, above, these decisions should be communicated to the specifications writer by notations in the Drawings and Specifications Outline, so there will be no confusion and no duplication.

It is of particular importance that the nomenclature used in the drawings match that being used in the specifications. The identifying words may be synonymous, but they can be confusing when, for example, (1) the drawing note reads "precast concrete" while the specifications read "prestressed," or (2) the drawing note refers to a "frieze" while the specifications refer to a "cornice," or (3) the drawings call for "galvanized iron" while the specifications state "galvanized steel," or (4) the drawings are labeled "folding door" while the specifications call it a "folding partition." Even if the draftor and the specifications writer fully understand what is meant by the other, the builder, the subcontractors, and the suppliers may all be confused.

Thus, the drawings and specifications must work together fluently, which is to say the draftors and the specifications writer must keep aware of the work of the other. Properly used, the Drawings and Specifications Outline (see Figure 1-3) should be of great assistance to the drafting staff in communicating with the specifications writer. In turn, the project captain and the draftors should review the specifications on their completion to verify that the intent of the drawings has been carried through. In the process of reading the specifications for the set of drawings they have just produced, the draftors will become increasingly aware of the interrelationship of these contract documents.

SCHEDULES

Schedules are a convenient method for listing variable conditions. Most projects require schedules for room finishes, for doors, sometimes for windows, and for other variable items. The office should establish a standard blank form for each of these schedules which can be edited and traced for each project.

On completion of a roughed out schedule, all lines can be traced on the back of the finish tracing sheet—regular lines in pencil; borders, division lines, and every fifth horizontal line through the body of the schedule in heavy ink. Extra lines should be provided in case additions are made to the schedule. All information can then be lettered and symbolized on the face of the sheet, and corrections to any of the information can easily be made without disturbing the lines which are on the back.

Generally, locating the schedule in an upper sheet corner (upper left corner when occurring with a floor plan) is space-saving and convenient, and a schedule is most effective when located on the same sheet as the drawing to which it relates; for example:

Room finish schedule with floor plan

Door schedule with floor plan

Window schedule with exterior elevations or with window details

ROOM IDENTIFICATION AND FINISHES

A satisfactory identification system for scheduling, detailing, and specifying requires that every room and space be numbered in logical order. Unless the owner has established a numbering system which must be followed, the numbering should begin at the main entrance and continue room by room in a logical, easy-to-follow sequence; the traffic arteries or common spaces numbered first, followed by the rooms, generally in a clockwise sequence, as in Figure 6-7.

For distinctive identification, the room numbers should be enclosed by an oval and should follow the floor levels with these series:

B1, B2, etc., for basement

101, 102, etc., for lowest main floor

201, 202, etc., for second floor

Continue similarly for additional floor levels

Since stairs connect more than one level, they should be numbered S1, S2, etc.—the same number applicable to the full stair height.

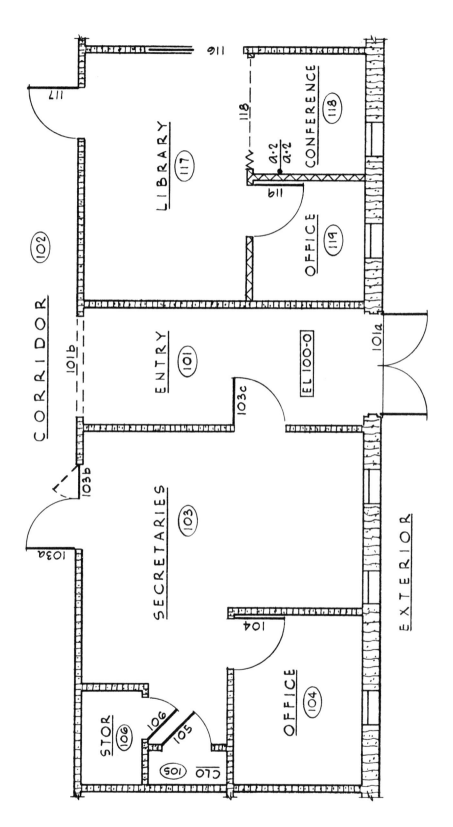

FIGURE 6-7 ROOM- AND DOOR-NUMBERING SYSTEM IN PLAN.

Figure 6-8 illustrates a room finish schedule which observes the following principles:

1. Room names are optional. They may be included as a convenient reference, but the room numbers are sufficient as long as the room names appear on the floor plan.

2. Although the basement and first- and second-floor rooms are shown on a combined schedule (as a convenience in illustrating the principle of room numbering sequence), a separate room finish schedule should be provided with each separate floor plan.

3. A finish designation, such as paint, paneling, and fabric, is incomplete unless the substrate is also designated; for example, "fabric on gypsum drywall."

4. Shaded (penciled in) portions of the appropriate boxes indicate the walls to receive the various finishes, the orientation coinciding with the respective floor plan. A circle designates a finish that applies to all areas.

5. Unnecessary abbreviations should be avoided, and if any special abbreviations are necessary, they must be listed at the bottom of the schedule.

6. The approximate ceiling height is noted rather than the actual height, which may include fractions of an inch.

7. The "remarks" column should include only those items which cannot otherwise be easily identified by the schedule or by other drawing notes or details.

When a residence or other project contains few rooms or has few finishes, these may be conveniently indicated by a simplified room finish schedule, as in Figure 6-9. In this schedule, the finish assignments are each indicated by abbreviations, and all abbreviations should be listed following the schedule for the convenience of the reader. The four columns of orientation for the walls may be limited to one column when there is only one type of wall finish per room. Although this type of schedule has many limitations, it is quite flexible and can be quickly produced for uncomplicated projects.

C ROOM FINISH SCHEDULE

Legend: SHADED PORTIONS INDICATE AREAS TO RECEIVE FINISH (compass N/E/S/W symbol) — ● FINISH ALL AREAS

Room	Room Name	Floor: UNP CONCRETE	Floor: QUARRY TILE	Floor: CARPET	Floor: VINYL ASB TILE	Base: 4" TOPSET VINYL COVE	Base: 4" STRAIGHT VINYL	Base: QUARRY TILE	Wainscot: CERAMIC TILE ON GDW, 5' HT	Wainscot: STR FACING TILE, 5-4 HT	Wainscot: WOOD PNL ON GDW, 4-4 HT	Walls: UNP CONCRETE	Walls: PNT LCMU (BLOCK)	Walls: FACE BRICK	Walls: PNT GDW (DRYWALL)	Walls: PREFINISHED PLYWOOD	Walls: PNT PLASTER	Walls: GLASS WINDOW WALL	Walls: FABRIC ON GDW	Walls: UNP GDW	Columns: UNP CONCRETE	Columns: PNT GDW ON FURRING	Columns: FABRIC ON PLASTER	Ceiling: ACOUSTIC PANELS	Ceiling: TX PNT ON GDW	Ceiling: UNF GDW	Ceiling: PNT STEEL	Ceiling: UNP CONCRETE	APX HEIGHT	REMARKS
B1	MECHANICAL	●										◪	◪								●							●	12-0	
B2	STORAGE	●											●								●						●		12-0	
101	LOBBY		●					◪						◪				◪											9-0	
102	RECEPTION			●			●				●			●	◪									●					←	
103	CORRIDOR			●			●								●							●			●					
104	OFFICE			●			●								●									●						TF WD CBT
105	OFFICE			●			●								◪	◪									●				→	
106	MEN				●	●			●										●				●		●				9-0	
107	WOMEN				●	●			●										●				●		●				8-0	
108	KITCHEN		●					●		●							●							●					8-0	TF WD CBTS, PLAM CTR
109	CONFERENCE			●			●									●									●				9-0	
201	FUTURE OFFICES	●																		●						●			9-0	
202	CORRIDOR	●																		●						●			9-0	
203	FUTURE OFFICES	●																		●						●			9-0	
S1	STAIR NO. 1			●			●										●								●				VARIES	
S2	STAIR NO. 2			●			●										●								●				VARIES	

FIGURE 6-8 ROOM FINISH SCHEDULE.

B ROOM FINISH SCHEDULE

ROOM NO.	FLOOR	BASE	WALLS N	WALLS E	WALLS S	WALLS W	CEILING	APX HEIGHT	REMARKS
101	QT	QT	PNT/GDW	PNT/GDW	PNT/GDW	PNT/GDW	PNT/GDW	8-0	
102	CONC	VIN	PNT/LCMU	PNT/LCMU	PNT/LCMU	PNT/LCMU	AC/PNLS	9-0	
103	VAT	↕	↕	↕	VF/PLAS	VF/PLAS	↕	↕	TF WOOD CBTS
104	VAT				VF/GDW	VF/GDW			
105	VAT	↕	PNT/LCMU	PNT/LCMU	PNT/LCMU	PNT/LCMU	↕	9-0	
106	CONC	VIN	UNP/CONC	UNP/CONC	UNP/CONC	UNP/CONC	AC/PNLS	10-0	

ABBREVIATIONS ABOVE:

AC ACOUSTIC	GDW GYPSUM DRYWALL	PNLS PANELS	UNP UNPAINTED
APX APPROXIMATE	LCMU LIGHTWEIGHT CONC MASONRY UNITS	PNT PAINTED	VAT VINYL ASBESTOS TILE
CBTS CABINETS		QT QUARRY TILE	VF VINYL FABRIC
CONC CONCRETE	N NORTH	S SOUTH	VIN VINYL
E EAST	PLAS PLASTER	TF TRANSPARENT FINISH	W WEST

FIGURE 6-9 ROOM FINISH SCHEDULE FOR SIMPLER PROJECTS.

DOORS AND FRAMES

Figure 6-10 illustrates the floor-plan indications for various types of doors and openings. Generally, hinged doors are best illustrated full open, but a 45° or smaller opening is permissible when space is limited. The door leaf should be drawn with a single bold line and the swing described by a light line.

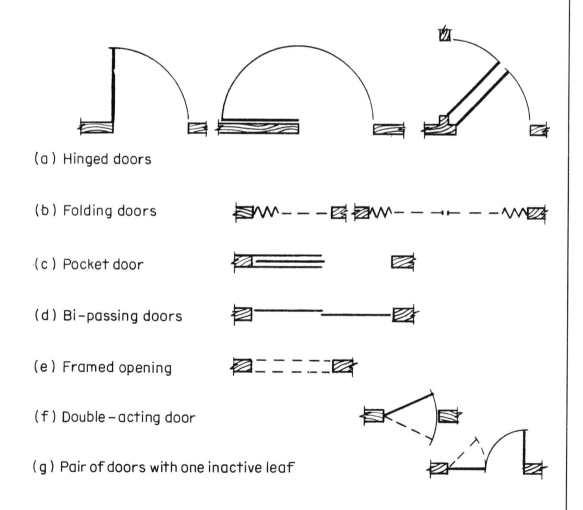

(a) Hinged doors

(b) Folding doors

(c) Pocket door

(d) Bi-passing doors

(e) Framed opening

(f) Double-acting door

(g) Pair of doors with one inactive leaf

FIGURE 6-10 INDICATING DOORS IN PLAN.

Since both doors and framed openings require frames, *doors and frames* should be identified in the numbering system and included in a combined "door and frame schedule." As in Figure 6-7, the doors should be identified by the same number as the room into which the door opens, except that doors opening from a room to a corridor should be given the room number. Framed openings may be numbered with either of the rooms they adjoin. When a room contains more than one door, the door numbers should be designated *a, b, c,* etc. Relating these openings to the room by the numbering system makes for convenient indexing whereby any door opening may be quickly found; and an individual number for each door and opening is a decided benefit to the builder and suppliers in scheduling doors, frames, and hardware and is a benefit to those who will need to check these schedules.

An exception to this numbering system may be made for a residence or other building when there are so few variances in the materials and types of doors and frames that they can be conveniently indicated by the specifications or by drawing notes and details. In such cases, the doors and frames may be indicated as shown in Figure 6-11 (and as similarly shown in Figure 2-7), which has the advantage of identifying the door width and height on the

FIGURE 6-11 DOOR AND FRAME INDICATION FOR SIMPLER PROJECTS.

floor plan, a particularly convenient method for residences where each opening must be job-framed. When this method is used, the indication system (Figure 6-11) must be illustrated on the drawings and preferably on a floor-plan sheet.

Shower doors, cabinet doors, and toilet partition doors are part of an assembly, and should be described in the specifications. They are not to be numbered on the plans or included in the schedule. However, a full-size door with normal hardware used in conjunction with a cabinet should be numbered and scheduled.

Figure 6-12 illustrates a door and frame schedule which observes the following principles:

1. Opening numbers corresponding with those on the floor plans.

2. Door and frame elevation types, frame sections, and lintel types are referenced to the supporting details or schedules by the *boxed* reference number.

3. Both composition and finishes are stated.

4. The "specials" column permits special hardware and other variable conditions to be indicated. Further description of hardware should be relegated to the specifications or to a hardware schedule.

5. Circles identify the applicable conditions, and to permit ease of change during the drawing process they should not be filled in solidly with pencil until all anticipated changes have been completed.

Special abbreviations may be needed in the schedule to identify glazing types, and these must each be explained at the bottom of the schedule.

Typical details of doors and frames are indicated in Figure 6-13. Similar details for each project will need to be developed illustrating the door elevation types (as in *a*), the frame elevation types (as in *b*), a typical profile section for sections (as in *c*), and jamb sections (as in *d*)—occasionally head sections will also be necessary—illustrating typical installation conditions. In most cases finishes and finish dimensions need not be designated, for these

A DOOR and FRAME SCHEDULE

OPENING NUMBER	SIZE	THICKNESS	DOOR TYPE [3C]	DOOR COMPOSITION	DOOR FINISH	FRAME ELEVATION TYPE [3D]	FRAME SECTION [3E]	FRAME COMPOSITION	FRAME FINISH	LINTEL TYPE [4G]	GLAZING DOOR	GLAZING SIDELIGHT	GLAZING TRANSOM	SPECIALS
101	PR 3-0x7-0	1¾	1	HOLLOW ALUMINUM	PREFINISHED	4	–	HOLLOW ALUMINUM	PREFINISHED	2	¼T	¼T	¼T	HEAD CLOSER; PANIC DEVICE; THRESHOLD
102	2-8x7-0	1¾	2	HOLLOW STEEL	PAINT	1	1	HOLLOW STEEL	PAINT	1				
103a	2-8x7-0	1¾	4	HOLLOW STEEL	PAINT	1	2	HOLLOW STEEL	PAINT		¼W			LABEL ASSEMBLY CLASS B
103b	3-4x7-0	1¾	2	WOOD, SOLID CORE	TRANSPARENT	1	7	HOLLOW STEEL	PAINT					
104	2-6x7-0	1¾	2	WOOD, SOLID CORE	TRANSPARENT	1	7	HOLLOW STEEL	PAINT					
105	2-0x7-0	1⅜	2	WOOD, HOLLOW CORE	TRANSPARENT	1	8	WOOD	TRANSPARENT	4				
106	2-6x7-0	1⅜	2	WOOD, HOLLOW CORE	TRANSPARENT	1	7/8	HOLLOW STEEL	PAINT		⁷⁄₃₂S			
107a	3-0x8-0	1¾	5	WOOD, SOLID CORE	TRANSPARENT	1	4	HOLLOW STEEL	PAINT	G				HEAD CLOSER
107b	2-8x7-0	1¾	2	HOLLOW STEEL	PAINT	1	1	HOLLOW STEEL	PAINT					
108	2-6x6-8	1¾	2	WOOD, HOLLOW CORE	TRANSPARENT	1	8	HOLLOW STEEL	PAINT					
109	PR 3-0x6-8			WOOD SLAT, FOLDING	PREFINISHED	2	7	WOOD	TRANSPARENT / PREFINISHED	2				
110	3-0x7-0	1¾	2	WOOD, LABELED	TRANSPARENT	3	5	HOLLOW STEEL	PAINT	1				LABEL ASSEMBLY CLASS B; HEAD CLOSER

144

FIGURE 6-12   DOOR AND FRAME SCHEDULE.

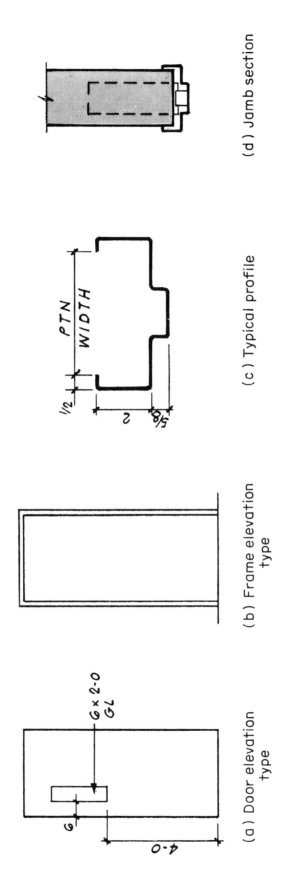

(d) Jamb section

(c) Typical profile

PTN WIDTH

1/2

2

5/8

(b) Frame elevation type

(a) Door elevation type

G x 2-0
GL

G

4-0

FIGURE 6-13 TYPICAL DETAILS OF DOORS AND FRAMES.

145

should be verified by the supplier and later by the builder from the construction information on the plans and schedules. A prepared set of office standard detail sheets will prove quite time-saving for the tracing of these rather standardized and simple details. They should be traced near the door and frame schedule when possible.

WINDOWS

Simplified window sections, as in Figure 6-3a, will be necessary to indicate the general installation requirements, but in the floor plans the windows should be indicated only diagrammatically. Several types of these window diagrams are illustrated in Figure 6-14.

For projects that have few variations in types and details of windows, a schedule may be superfluous. A schedule is advisable when there is a considerable variety of window types and details (see Figure 6-15), with the *elevation marks* coinciding with the square-enclosed number identifying each window on the exterior elevations, as in Figure 4-12. If the scale of the exterior elevation is quite small, window elevation types in a larger scale, as in Figure 6-15b, should be drawn adjacent to and coordinated with the window schedule. Applicable details of the window heads, jambs, and sills may be included in the schedule under the "details" column by using the reference system for identification of these details.

LINTELS

In most buildings there are lintels spanning each of the many openings in walls and partitions. In large projects, the lintels are customarily detailed and scheduled in the structural drawings. For simpler projects, especially those utilizing bearing walls, the lintels may be designed by the structural engineer and detailed and scheduled either in the structural or in the architectural drawings, depending on convenience. But in most projects, there are a

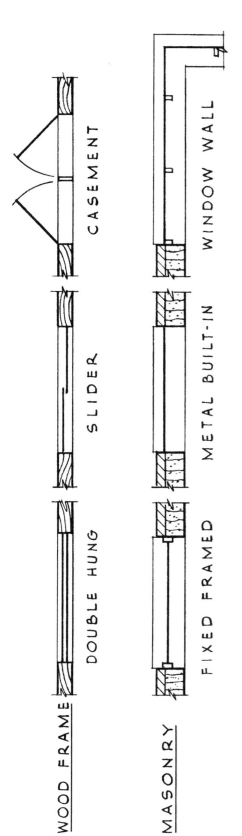

WOOD FRAME

DOUBLE HUNG SLIDER CASEMENT

MASONRY

FIXED FRAMED METAL BUILT-IN WINDOW WALL

FIGURE 6-14   WINDOW DIAGRAMS IN PLAN.

(b) Window type

A	WINDOW SCHEDULE								
EL MARK	WINDOW TYPE	DIMENSIONS		DETAILS			WINDOW GLASS	PANELS	
		MO WIDTH	HEIGHT	HEAD	JAMB	SILL		INSULATED	NON-INS
1	n	3-4	10-0	9A2	9A3	9A4	7/32 GRAY	●	
2	b	6-0	9-4	9A7	9A3	9A5	1/4 PP		●
3	c	4-0	9-6	9A1	9A6	9A4	1/4 T	●	
4	a	1-4	8-0	9A1	9A8	9A5	DSA	●	

(a) Window schedule

FIGURE 6-15   WINDOW-SCHEDULE AND WINDOW-TYPE IDENTIFICATION.

G MISCELLANEOUS LINTELS

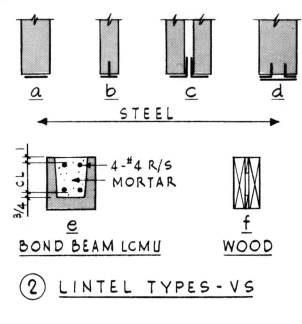

DRAWING OR SCHEDULE MARK	TYPE	NOMINAL SIZE OR STRUCTURAL SHAPE
		LINTEL SCHEDULE
L-1	a	PL 5/16 × 7
L-2	b	MT4 × 8.5
L-3	c	2∠ 3½ × 3½ × 5/16
L-4	d	2∠3×3×5/16 / PL ¼ ×11
L-5	e	8 × 8
L-6	f	8 × 16
L-7	g	2 - 2 × 8

② LINTEL TYPES - VS

PROVIDE LINTEL FOR EACH WALL & PARTITION OPENING. UNLESS INDICATED BY DWG OR SCHEDULE, PROVIDE LINTEL CONSISTENT WITH WALL CONDITION & SIMILAR DETAILS.

BEARING LENGTH EA END AT LEAST 1" PER FOOT OF CLEAR SPAN AND NOT LESS THAN 1½" ON WOOD, 2½" ON STEEL, 4" ON MASONRY AND 8" FOR BOND BEAMS, UNLESS NOTED.

PLUG WELD OR BOLT BACK-TO-BACK STL ∠S WITHIN 6" OF ENDS & 2-0 MAX BTW. CONT WELD ∠S TO PLS.

FIGURE 6-16 MISCELLANEOUS LINTELS.

myriad of doors and other openings in interior partitions that require lintels, and these may be difficult to indicate unless they are incorporated with the architectural drawings. Figure 6-16 indicates a typical schedule and accompanying section types and related notations for miscellaneous lintels, as they might appear in the architectural drawings. Those lintels occurring over doors and framed openings can be identified from the door and frame schedule (see Figure 6-12). Other miscellaneous lintels should be noted and referenced on the floor plans at their specific locations.

SOIL-BORING LOG

The log of the soil borings which have been drilled, analyzed, and reported by the soils engineer should be shown on the drawings, in a manner similar to that shown in Figure 6-17. Preferably, they should appear adjacent to the site plan for ease of referencing the

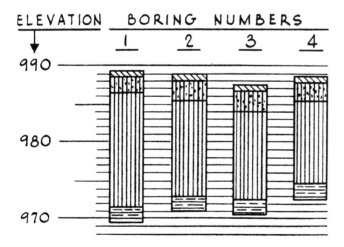

FIGURE 6-17 SOIL-BORING LOG.

boring locations and the relative grades. The symbols and descriptions of soil materials used in the legend should be those same symbols and descriptions furnished in the report of the soils engineer.

PARTITIONS

Indicating the partition construction by the appropriate hatching symbols on the floor plans and designating the finishes in the room finish schedule may not be fully adequate for the project that involves many variables in the construction and finishes of the partitions. Some of the partitions may extend only to the ceilings, while others may extend through the ceiling to the superstructure. Some partitions may have different plies and thicknesses of drywall on one or both faces for different requirements of fire-retardance, and some may contain sound blankets. These and other differences must be made comprehensible, preferably by an explanation diagram, as in Figure 6-18, appearing prominently on the drawings.

A majority of the concrete-block partitions, gypsum drywall partitions, etc., will be similar in construction throughout the project, and these may be detailed as a *general type,* as in the vertical sections of Figure 6-18. Thus unless a partition symbol occurs on the floor plan, as in Room 118 of Figure 6-7, the builder can presume a partition is one of the general types. Where a partition symbol does occur, it reveals special conditions both below and above the ceiling, following the indications in Figure 6-18. The legend may be modified to include all the variables that will be necessary to describe the special conditions of the partitioning system.

MARKED PRINTS

Attempting to remember all the necessary corrections and improvements that are made as the drawings are developed is

A PARTITION INDICATIONS

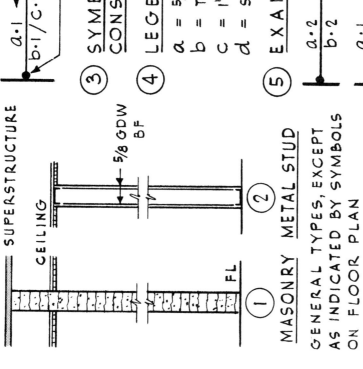

SUPERSTRUCTURE

CEILING

⁵/₈ GDW
BF

FL

MASONRY   METAL STUD
① ②

a·1 — CLG TO SUPERSTRUCTURE
b·1/C·2 — FLOOR TO CEILING
— DOT ON PARTITION FACE

③ SYMBOL FOR SPECIAL PARTITION
CONSTRUCTION

④ LEGEND

a = ⁵/₈" GDW
b = TWO PLY ¹/₂" GDW
c = 1" GDW SHAFT LINER
d = SOUND BLANKET

⑤ EXAMPLES

$\dfrac{a·2}{b·2}$ = $\dfrac{⁵/₈" \text{ GDW, 2 SIDES, ABV CLG}}{\text{TWO PLY } ¹/₂" \text{ GDW, 2 SIDES, BLW CLG}}$

$\dfrac{a·1}{b·1/C·1}$ = $\dfrac{⁵/₈" \text{ GDW 1 SIDE, ABV CLG}}{\text{TWO PLY } ¹/₂" \text{ GDW, OPP SIDE}\ \}\text{BLW}}$ 1" GDW SHAFT LINER, DOT SIDE} CLG

a·2·d = $\dfrac{\text{NONE ABV CLG}}{⁵/₈" \text{ GDW 2 SIDES, SOUND BLANKET}}$

GENERAL TYPES, EXCEPT
AS INDICATED BY SYMBOLS
ON FLOOR PLAN

FIGURE 6-18   PARTITION INDICATIONS.

ineffective. For efficiency, all corrections, ideas for improvement, and incomplete items should be noted in red (pencil or ink) on one set of whiteprints. No more than *one set* thus marked should be in use, and as these red-marked items are acted upon, they should be crossed out with a transparent yellow marker. When all corrections and pick-ups have been completed, the set should be destroyed, and another set of marking prints begun, on which the ever-developing improvements and needed corrections can be progressively recorded.

STANDARD DETAILS

Every office develops and adopts details of construction which, even though some may be unique, become standards with the office through repetitive use. Unless the project calls for a special design or application, developing a new detail will be time-consuming and unnecessary when an experience-proven detail would work as well. Therefore, the *standard details* of the office should be kept available in some form for referencing and for tracing. A loose-leaf notebook containing reproductions of these standards, divided into categories for ease of indexing, can be a practical aid to draftors for both reference and tracing. This book must be kept up to date as the details are improved.

Although few would question the efficiency of using standard details in some form, many will debate the method by which this can be implemented. There are several notable methods in practice, including:

1. Producing the drawings in two volumes—one containing site plans, floor plans, exterior elevations, schedules, and specialized details; the other a booklet of standard details keyed to the main drawing sheets

2. Selecting the applicable standard details for the project, then indexing and printing them to appear on 8½ × 11″ sheets as an appendix to the specifications

3. Inserting with each set of drawings one or more regular-size drawing sheets which include only standard details, crossing out the details that are not applicable to the project

4. Reproducing the standard details on transfer film, either by preprinting or by photocopying (see Chapter 7), and adhering these details to the back of the drawings, thereby being able to draft additional information on the drawing face

5. Applying paste-up details on the face of an opaque white drawing sheet, then photoreproducing to make a drafting film tracing (see Chapter 7)

Considering the complexities of detail coordination and the handling and filing of the contract documents, and considering the simplicity and clarity of drawings that a quality project deserves and that a builder has the right to expect, many firms believe the more appropriate, comprehensible, and time-saving method is to produce all the drawings specifically for the project, including tracing the applicable standard details on the drawings where they apply rather than including them in a separate booklet or in the specifications.

Details such as doorframe sections, door panel elevations, floor and base types, walks, curbs and gutters, and masonry wall joints and corners are so typical that they are logical candidates for the standard detail system. There are relatively few other details that are so typical that they can be used on repeat projects without considerable editing, and many will have to be redrawn in whole or in part. Therefore, the use of *standard details should not be considered a panacea,* for it takes expert draftors to select and edit the details in coordination with the specific project, and that same expertise might be used to produce the same drawings almost as rapidly by tracing them or by using the office standards as a reference. *The speed of producing any construction drawing is more directly related to the technical knowledge (and thus the training) of the draftor than to any system of drafting aids.*

STANDARD ABBREVIATIONS AND SYMBOLS

The abbreviations in Table 6-1, the architectural symbols in Figure 6-19, and the mechanical and electrical symbols in Figure 6-20 are

TABLE 6-1 Architectural Abbreviations

AB	anchor bolt	CCG	concrete curb and gutter	E	east
ABV	above			EA	each
AC	acoustical	CEM	cement	EB	expansion bolt
A/C	air conditioning	CF	cubic feet	EC	electrical contract(or)
ACT	acoustical tile	CHBD	chalkboard	EJ	expansion joint
AD	area drain	CIP	cast-iron pipe	EL	elevation
ADH	adhesive	CJT	construction joint	ELEC	electric(al)
ADJ	adjustable	CK	calk(ing)	ELEV	elevator
AFF	above finished floor	CLG	ceiling	ENC	enclose; enclosure
AL	aluminum	CLO	closet	EOI	except as otherwise indicated
ALT	alternate	CL	clear(ance)		
ANC	anchor; anchorage	CMU	concrete masonry unit(s)	EP	electrical panel
AP	access panel			EQP	equipment
APX	approximate	CO	cleanout; company	EXC	excavate
ARCH	architect(ural)	COL	column	EXG	existing
ASB	asbestos	CONC	concrete	EXH	exhaust
ASPH	asphalt	CONT	continue; continuous	EXP	exposed
AUTO	automatic	CONTR	contract(or)	EXT	exterior
		CORR	corrugated		
		CPG	coping	F	fahrenheit; face
BD	board	CPR	copper	FA	fresh air
BBD	bulletin board	CPT	carpet(ed)	FB	face brick
BF	both faces	CR	crushed	FBD	fiberboard
BLDG	building	CRS	course(s)	FD	floor drain
BLK	block	CSK/S	countersunk screw	FDN	foundation
BLKG	blocking	CT	ceramic tile	FDR	folding door
BLW	below	CTR	counter; center	FE	fire extinguisher
BM	beam; bench mark	CUH	cabinet unit heater	FHS	flathead screw
BPL	bearing plate	CW	cold water. concrete walk	FH	fire hose station
BR	bedroom			FIN	finish
BRG	bearing	CY	cubic yard	FJT	flush joint
BRK	brick			FL	floor
BRKT	bracket	DBL	double	F/L	flowline
BRZ	bronze	DC	drainage conductor	FLCO	floor cleanout
BSMT	basement	DEPT	department	FL/EL	floor elevation
BTM	bottom	DF	drinking fountain	FLG	flashing
BTN	batten	DIA	diameter	FLUR	fluorescent
BTW	between	DIM	dimension	FLX	flexible
BVL	beveled	DIV	division; divider	FOF	face of finish
BW	both ways	DL	dead load	FPL	floor plate
		DN	down	FR	frame(d); framing
		DP	deep	FS	full size, far side
C	channel	DR	door	FT(')	foot
CB	catch basin	DTA	dovetail anchor	FTG	footing
CBT	cabinet	DTL	detail	FUR	furred; furring
C-C	center to center	DWG	drawing	FURN	furnace

154

FUT	future	LF	linear foot	OHG	overhang
FV	face (facade) view	LL	live load	OPG	opening
FXT	fixture	LLH	long leg horizontal	OPP	opposite
		LLV	long leg vertical		
G	gas	LR	living room	PBD	particle board
GA	gage; gauge	LT	light	PBG	plumbing
GB	grab bar	LTL	lintel	PC	piece
GC	general contract(or)	LVR	louver	PCC	precast concrete
GDW	gypsum drywall	LWC	lightweight concrete	PCF	pounds per cubic foot
GL	glass; glazing			PED	pedestal
GS	galvanized steel	MAS	masonry	PERF	perforate(d)
GSP	galvanized steel pipe	MAX	maximum	PFB	prefabricate(d)
GF	granular fill	MC	mechanical contract(or)	PL	plate; property line
		MECH	mechanical	PLF	pounds per lineal foot
HC	hollow core	MED	medicine cabinet; medium	PLAM	plastic laminate
HDW	hardware	MFD	manufactured	PLAS	plaster
HK	hook(s)	MFR	manufacturer	PLS	plastic
HM	hollow metal	MIN	minimum	PNL	panel
HOR	horizontal	MIR	mirror	PNT	paint(ed)
HP	horsepower	MISC	miscellaneous	PR	pair
HR	handrail; hour	MLD	molding	PROJ	project; projected
HT	height	MO	masonry opening	PS	plan section
HTG	heating	MOD	modular	PSC	prestressed concrete
HVAC	heating/ventilating/air conditioning	MOV	movable	PSF	pounds per square foot
HW	hot water	M/RFG	membrane roofing	PSI	pounds per square inch
HYD	hydrant	MS	masonry shelf		
		MTL	metal	PT	part; point
INCL	include(d); including	MUL	mullion	PTN	partition
ID	inside diameter			PVCP	polyvinyl chloride pipe
IN.(″)	inch	N	north		
INS	insulate(d); insulation	NIC	not in contract	PVMT	pavement
INT	interior	NO.	number	PWD	plywood
INV	invert	NOM	nominal		
		NRC	noise reduction coefficient	QT	quarry tile
JC	janitor's closet	NS	near side		
JST	joist	NTS	not to scale	R	radius; riser
JT	joint			RA	return air
		OA	overall	RBT	rabbet(ed)
KIT.	kitchen	OBS	obscure	R/C	reinforced concrete
		OC	on center(s)	RD	roof drain
L	long; length	OD	outside diameter	REF	refer(ence)
LAB	laboratory	OFF	office	REG	register
LAV	lavatory	OH	overhead	REQ	required
LCMU	lightweight concrete masonry unit(s)				

155

(Continued)

TABLE 6-1 Architectural Abbreviations (*Continued*)

REV	revise; revision	SYM	symmetry; symmetrical	WC	water closet
RFG	roofing			WD	wood
RFR	refrigerator	SYN	synthetic	WDO	window
RHS	roundhead screw	SYS	system	WF	wood framing
RL	rail(ing)			WG	wired glass
RM	room	T	tee; toilet; tread	WH	water heater
RMV	remove	TB	towel bar; tackboard	WO	window opening
RO	rough opening	TC	top of curb	W/O	without
RPM	revolutions per minute	TEL	telephone	WP	waterproof(ing)
		TF	transparent finish	WPT	working point
R/S	reinforcing steel	T&G	tongue and groove	WSCT	wainscot
RT	rubber tile	THK	thick(ness)	WWF	welded wire fabric
RVS	reverse	THR	threshold		
R/W	retaining wall	TPTN	toilet partition		
		T/SL	top of slab		
S	south; sink	T/STL	top of steel		Symbols as abbreviations:
SB	splashblock	TV	television	$\angle$	angle
SC	solid core	T/W	top of wall	₵	centerline
SCH	schedule	TX	textured	d	penny
SCT	structural clay tile	TYP	typical	$\perp$	perpendicular
SD	storm drain	TZ	terrazzo	⌀	round; diameter
SDG	siding			⊡	square
SEC	section	UH	unit heater		
SF	square foot	UNF	unfinished		
SH	shelf; shelving; shower	UNP	unpainted		Metric symbols
		UR	urinal	A	ampere
SHT	sheet			°C	degree Celsius
SIM	similar	V	volt	cd	candela
SKL	skylight	VAT	vinyl asbestos tile	g	gram
SOF	soffit	VB	vinyl base; vapor barrier	ha	hectare
SPC	space; spacer			J	joule
SPEC	specification(s)	VCP	vitrified clay pipe	K	kelvin
SPK	speaker	VENT	ventilator	kg	kilogram
SQ	square	VERT	vertical	kJ	kilojoule
SST	stainless steel	VEST	vestibule	km	kilometer
STC	sound transmission coefficient	VF	vinyl fabric	kN	kilonewton
		VIN	vinyl	kW	kilowatt
STD	standard	VNR	veneer	L	liter
STL	steel	VS	vertical section	lx	lux
STO	storage	VT	vinyl tile	m	meter
STR	structure; structural			mm	millimeter
SUS	suspended			N	newton
SW	switch	W	west; width; water	s	second
SY	square yard	W/	with	W	watt
				V	volt

PLAN OR SECTION

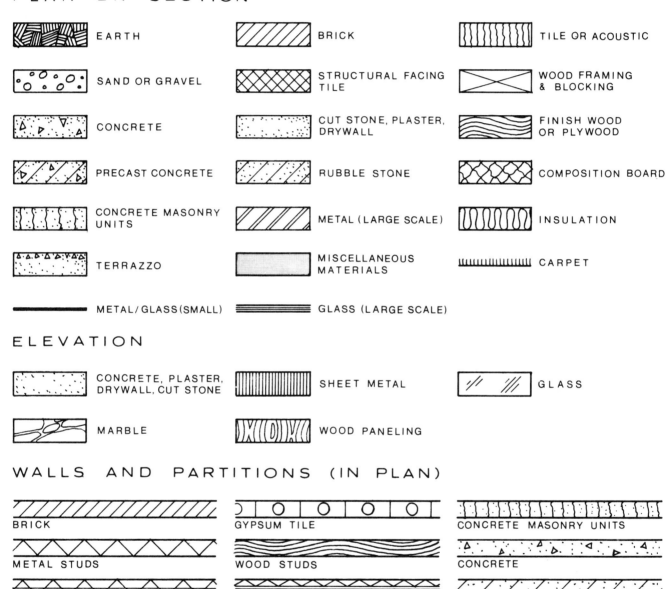

EARTH	BRICK	TILE OR ACOUSTIC
SAND OR GRAVEL	STRUCTURAL FACING TILE	WOOD FRAMING & BLOCKING
CONCRETE	CUT STONE, PLASTER, DRYWALL	FINISH WOOD OR PLYWOOD
PRECAST CONCRETE	RUBBLE STONE	COMPOSITION BOARD
CONCRETE MASONRY UNITS	METAL (LARGE SCALE)	INSULATION
TERRAZZO	MISCELLANEOUS MATERIALS	CARPET

METAL/GLASS (SMALL)   GLASS (LARGE SCALE)

ELEVATION

CONCRETE, PLASTER, DRYWALL, CUT STONE	SHEET METAL	GLASS
MARBLE	WOOD PANELING	

WALLS AND PARTITIONS (IN PLAN)

BRICK	GYPSUM TILE	CONCRETE MASONRY UNITS
METAL STUDS	WOOD STUDS	CONCRETE
METAL STUDS & SOUND BLANKET	METAL STUDS – 2 SPACED ROWS	RUBBLE STONE
STRUCTURAL FACING TILE	STAGGERED WOOD STUDS & SOUND BLANKET	PREFAB PARTITIONS

FIGURE 6-19   ARCHITECTURAL SYMBOLS.

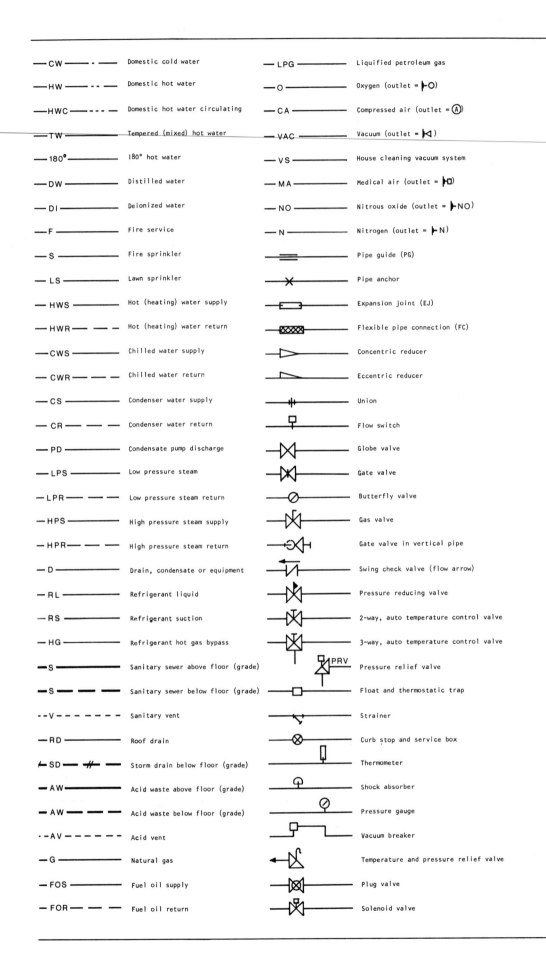

—CW—————·———	Domestic cold water
—HW———·· ———	Domestic hot water
—HWC—— - - - —	Domestic hot water circulating
—TW————————	Tempered (mixed) hot water
—180°———————	180° hot water
—DW————————	Distilled water
—DI————————	Deionized water
—F—————————	Fire service
—S—————————	Fire sprinkler
—LS————————	Lawn sprinkler
—HWS———————	Hot (heating) water supply
—HWR—— — — —	Hot (heating) water return
—CWS———————	Chilled water supply
—CWR—— — — —	Chilled water return
—CS————————	Condenser water supply
—CR—— — — —	Condenser water return
—PD————————	Condensate pump discharge
—LPS————————	Low pressure steam
—LPR—— — — —	Low pressure steam return
—HPS————————	High pressure steam supply
—HPR—— — — —	High pressure steam return
—D—————————	Drain, condensate or equipment
—RL————————	Refrigerant liquid
—RS————————	Refrigerant suction
—HG————————	Refrigerant hot gas bypass
▬S————————	Sanitary sewer above floor (grade)
▬S ▬ ▬ ▬ ▬	Sanitary sewer below floor (grade)
--V — — — — —	Sanitary vent
—RD————————	Roof drain
◄ SD ▬ —//— ▬	Storm drain below floor (grade)
▬AW———————	Acid waste above floor (grade)
▬AW ▬ — — —	Acid waste below floor (grade)
·-AV — — — — ·	Acid vent
—G—————————	Natural gas
—FOS————————	Fuel oil supply
—FOR—— — — —	Fuel oil return

—LPG————————	Liquified petroleum gas
—O—————————	Oxygen (outlet = ⊢O)
—CA————————	Compressed air (outlet = Ⓐ)
—VAC————————	Vacuum (outlet = ⋈)
—VS————————	House cleaning vacuum system
—MA————————	Medical air (outlet = ⊢□)
—NO————————	Nitrous oxide (outlet = ⊢NO)
—N—————————	Nitrogen (outlet = ⊢N)
	Pipe guide (PG)
	Pipe anchor
	Expansion joint (EJ)
	Flexible pipe connection (FC)
	Concentric reducer
	Eccentric reducer
	Union
	Flow switch
	Globe valve
	Gate valve
	Butterfly valve
	Gas valve
	Gate valve in vertical pipe
	Swing check valve (flow arrow)
	Pressure reducing valve
	2-way, auto temperature control valve
	3-way, auto temperature control valve
	Pressure relief valve
	Float and thermostatic trap
	Strainer
	Curb stop and service box
	Thermometer
	Shock absorber
	Pressure gauge
	Vacuum breaker
	Temperature and pressure relief valve
	Plug valve
	Solenoid valve

158

FIGURE 6-20 MECHANICAL AND ELECTRICAL SYMBOLS.

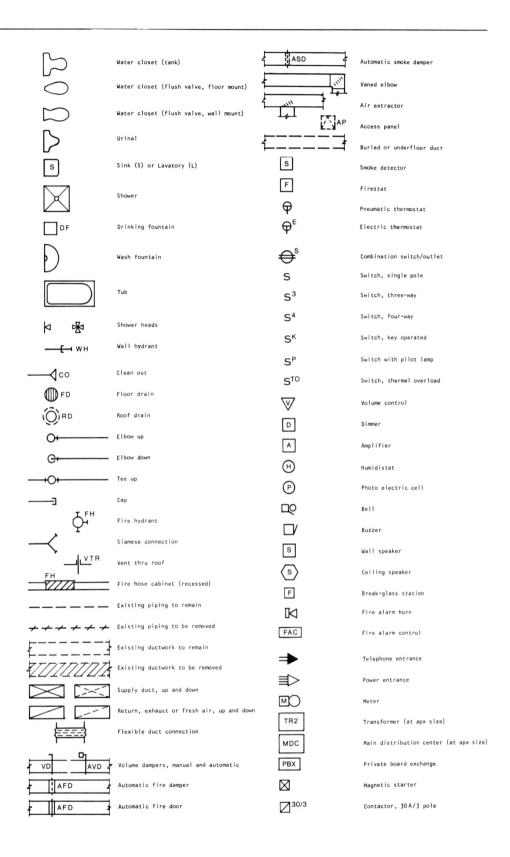

Symbol	Description
	Water closet (tank)
	Water closet (flush valve, floor mount)
	Water closet (flush valve, wall mount)
	Urinal
S	Sink (S) or Lavatory (L)
	Shower
DF	Drinking fountain
	Wash fountain
	Tub
	Shower heads
WH	Wall hydrant
CO	Clean out
FD	Floor drain
RD	Roof drain
	Elbow up
	Elbow down
	Tee up
	Cap
FH	Fire hydrant
	Siamese connection
VTR	Vent thru roof
FH	Fire hose cabinet (recessed)
	Existing piping to remain
	Existing piping to be removed
	Existing ductwork to remain
	Existing ductwork to be removed
	Supply duct, up and down
	Return, exhaust or fresh air, up and down
	Flexible duct connection
VD AVD	Volume dampers, manual and automatic
AFD	Automatic fire damper
AFD	Automatic fire door

Symbol	Description
ASD	Automatic smoke damper
	Vaned elbow
	Air extractor
AP	Access panel
	Buried or underfloor duct
S	Smoke detector
F	Firestat
	Pneumatic thermostat
E	Electric thermostat
S	Combination switch/outlet
S	Switch, single pole
S³	Switch, three-way
S⁴	Switch, four-way
Sᴷ	Switch, key operated
Sᴾ	Switch with pilot lamp
Sᵀᴼ	Switch, thermal overload
V	Volume control
D	Dimmer
A	Amplifier
H	Humidistat
P	Photo electric cell
	Bell
	Buzzer
S	Wall speaker
S	Ceiling speaker
F	Break-glass station
	Fire alarm horn
FAC	Fire alarm control
	Telephone entrance
	Power entrance
M	Meter
TR2	Transformer (at apx size)
MDC	Main distribution center (at apx size)
PBX	Private board exchange
	Magnetic starter
30/3	Contactor, 30 A/3 pole

(Continued)

159

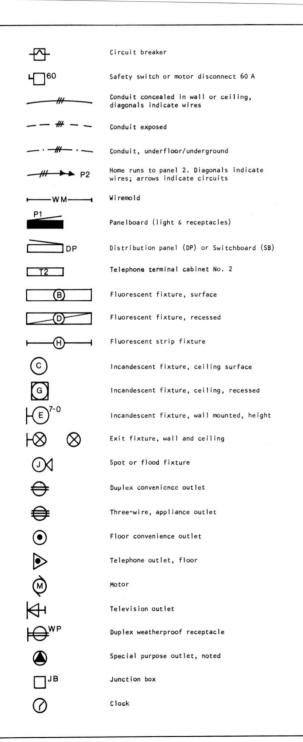

	Circuit breaker
	Safety switch or motor disconnect 60 A
	Conduit concealed in wall or ceiling, diagonals indicate wires
	Conduit exposed
	Conduit, underfloor/underground
	Home runs to panel 2. Diagonals indicate wires; arrows indicate circuits
	Wiremold
	Panelboard (light & receptacles)
	Distribution panel (DP) or Switchboard (SB)
	Telephone terminal cabinet No. 2
	Fluorescent fixture, surface
	Fluorescent fixture, recessed
	Fluorescent strip fixture
	Incandescent fixture, ceiling surface
	Incandescent fixture, ceiling, recessed
	Incandescent fixture, wall mounted, height
	Exit fixture, wall and ceiling
	Spot or flood fixture
	Duplex convenience outlet
	Three-wire, appliance outlet
	Floor convenience outlet
	Telephone outlet, floor
	Motor
	Television outlet
	Duplex weatherproof receptacle
	Special purpose outlet, noted
	Junction box
	Clock

FIGURE 6-20 MECHANICAL AND ELECTRICAL SYMBOLS. *(Continued)*

proposed as a practical standard for most architectural and related engineering offices.

The abbreviations are based on these principles:

1. Establishing a recognizable, abbreviated form of the word with the fewest possible letters
2. Using abbreviated forms that work well in architectural notations
3. Retaining traditional abbreviations wherever they can serve as well
4. Eliminating periods except after abbreviations that could be interpreted as another word, such as "no." and "off."
5. Including metric SI symbols

The architectural, mechanical, and electrical symbols are selected for ease of drawing and for clear representation. The architectural symbols are few in number since a limited palette is easier for the draftor and the builder to learn and because any possible ambiguities can be eliminated by the occasional material identification note on the drawings. For example, there are too many types of insulation to rely on identification by symbol alone; therefore, the standard insulation symbol identified by the note "INS BD" indicates insulation board, and the specifications can further describe the type and characteristics of the board. If more than one type of insulation board is used, the note should further identify the different types.

To be effective, the abbreviations and symbols must accompany the drawings as a convenient reference. They may be preprinted and inserted as an appendix to the specifications, or they may be preprinted as transfer films to be adhered to the drawing tracings. As appendixes, the abbreviations may be composed and photo-reduced for offset printing on a single 8½ × 11″ sheet, and the symbols (architectural, mechanical, and electrical) similarly produced on a second sheet. As appliqués on the drawing sheets, the abbreviations and symbols may be photoreproduced in small, readable size on transfer films—the abbreviations and architectural symbols applied to the architectural drawings (preferably on the first sheet), and the symbols divided and applied to the architectural, mechanical, and electrical sheets to which they relate. When the abbreviations appear as appendixes to the specifications, the drawings should bear a prominent reference note, such as, "ref specifications appendixes AP1 and AP2 for abbreviations and symbols."

Special projects may require special abbreviations and special symbols, which must then be noted and drawn as supplements on the drawings. When the standard abbreviations and symbols appear in the specifications appendix, the special abbreviations and symbols should be accompanied by a reference note, such as, "ref specifications appendixes AP1 and AP2 for other abbreviations and symbols."

The draftor can conserve considerable drawing and noting time by using appropriate symbols and abbreviations on the working drawings, presuming that an experienced builder will observe and be conversant with the symbol and abbreviation standards included in the specifications appendix and as supplemented on the drawings. However, the draftor should observe these cautions:

1. Don't depend on symbols alone to identify materials throughout the drawings; an occasional identification note will be necessary.

2. Avoid abbreviations for materials that appear only once or twice in the drawings (by saving four letters you may cause 40 readers to have to look something up).

3. Avoid abbreviations and identify symbols in presentation drawings or other drawings that will be read primarily by persons who cannot be expected to know the abbreviation/symbol system.

DRAWING THE FLOOR PLAN—A SEQUENCE

Unlike most of the other drawings, the architectural floor plan is better developed by a sequence that will avoid confusion and interferences as information is progressively entered on the tracing.

In the early stages, the plan will need to be an outline (free from unnecessary notes and dimensions) to be used as a base for the development of many other drawings, including structural, mechanical, and electrical ones. As the plan develops, dimensions, room names and numbers, notes, and other information will compete for space; and some information will not be available until further development of the details. Therefore, to permit an orderly development of the floor plan, this sequence of drawing is suggested to the draftor:

1. In very light line, establish (a) lines of exterior walls and structural columns, (b) critical openings for stairs, elevators, and escalators, (c) partitions, and (d) door openings, windows, and other openings.

2. In heavier line, outline the walls; partitions; doors, windows, and other openings; structural columns; stairs; elevators; and other prime elements.

3. Draw in windows, doors, and door swings.

4. Make a reproducible if the plan is to be used for the development of other drawing disciplines (mechanical, electrical, etc.).

5. For residences, indicate the light fixtures.

6. Establish the exterior dimensions and the dimension locations of the structural columns.

7. Establish the basic interior dimensions and follow with minor interior dimensions. Leave ample room space for room names and numbers, partitions symbols and other notes, symbols, and references.

8. Letter in room names and add the ellipse in which the room number will appear.

9. Prepare a "roughed out" reproducible sheet (or a whiteprint for small projects) on which the room and door numbers, special partition symbols, and special room finish notations are indicated; this sheet should be used as a working guide for coordinating with door and finish schedules and for marking up the many changes before the numbering and the notes are transferred to the final tracing.

10. For residences, draw in the electrical switches, switching connections, floor registers, wall registers, grilles, and ceiling registers (see Figure 2-7).

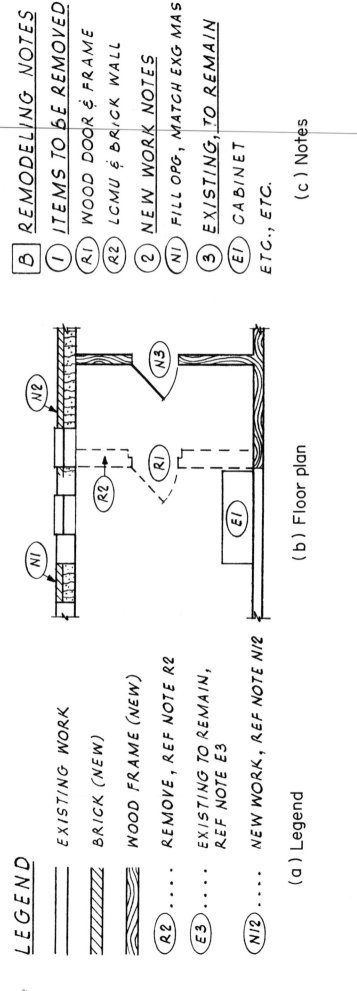

LEGEND

━━━━━━ EXISTING WORK

▨▨▨ BRICK (NEW)

〰〰〰 WOOD FRAME (NEW)

(R2) · · · · · REMOVE, REF NOTE R2

(E3) · · · · · EXISTING TO REMAIN, REF NOTE E3

(N12) · · · · · NEW WORK, REF NOTE N12

(a) Legend

REMODELING NOTES

| B | REMODELING NOTES |

① ITEMS TO BE REMOVED

(R1) WOOD DOOR & FRAME

(R2) LCMU & BRICK WALL

② NEW WORK NOTES

(N1) FILL OPG, MATCH EXG MAS

③ EXISTING, TO REMAIN

(E1) CABINET

ETC., ETC.

(c) Notes

(b) Floor plan

FIGURE 6-21 DRAWING AND NOTING FOR REMODELINGS.

11. Hatch in walls and partitions.

12. Line in divisions between floor materials and dot in changes of ceiling levels.

13. Indicate floor elevations (related to datum).

14. Show cutting planes of building sections.

15. Add room numbers, door numbers, and special partition indications.

16. Add notes and references to details.

REMODELINGS

Remodelings often require extensive instructional notes and a clear distinction between what is existing and what is new work. Floor plans drawn at the scale of $\frac{1}{8}'' = 1'-0''$ can seldom accommodate the necessary notes and indications. Floor plans drawn at the scale of $\frac{1}{4}'' = 1'-0''$ will usually be adequate, or $\frac{1}{8}''$ scale may be used for the general floor plan with supplementary larger-scale plans drawn of the areas with more complicated remodeling work.

Figure 6-21 details a method that simplifies the use of notes and symbols for remodelings. Different symbols are used to indicate that which is existing and that which will be new work. Most instructions are made in a column of remodeling notes, with each number corresponding to a number and an arrow on the floor plan. When the column of notes is extensive, typing (applied as a paste-on, as in Chapter 7) may be more efficient than hand lettering.

A room finish schedule may be required for extensive remodeling projects. A schedule, similar to Figure 6-8, will be workable when a "removal" column is added to the schedule. In the line space opposite each room, one or more numbers can be inserted under the "removal" column, with these numbers corresponding to an accompanying series of numbered notes designating and explaining the items to be removed.

7

PHOTODRAFTING AND REPRODUCTION PROCESSES

With the continual development and improvement of photographic equipment, films, and techniques, an ever-increasing number of technical options are becoming available to the draftor. Most projects contain many unique features that require careful planning and the use of conventional drafting to develop and detail. However, many of these projects may also contain elements that are highly repetitive, such as stacked floors in a high-rise building, repeated floor plans (with minor variations) in multiple-housing projects, and the standard details of the office. Additionally, the consulting engineers need copies of the floor plans as a base over which they can draw their disciplines.

Not every project can benefit from photodrafting and reproduction processes, but those with repetitive elements and those requiring a large number of copies of the documents are likely to discover that the process will permit completing the drawings phase on a time schedule better than that possible under conventional drafting methods, or at a better profit, or both. An objective of photodrafting and the resulting reproduction processes is to produce with the available staff more work of improved quality in the same (or even shorter) time span while utilizing a greater share of the time and personnel skills for developing and improving the design concept. Thus, the draftor is not to be replaced by the camera, but rather the techniques of the camera must become an additional skill to be mastered by the draftor in order to produce better drawings in less time.

DEFINITIONS

The explanations of these photo processes may become more meaningful with these general definitions:

Blueprint: The traditional direct-negative print, reproducing white lines on a blue/purple background.

Drafting paper: A fine grade 100 percent rag translucent paper for pencil and ink drafting.

Offset printing: Making ink reproductions by means of a rotary metal plate on an offset printing press.

Opaquing: "Touching out" the blemishes on a negative by painting on opaque liquid.

Overlay: A drafting film or paper covering—"overlaying"—the base sheet, illustrated with related disciplines.

Photocopier: A machine that instantly reproduces positive copies on photosensitive paper, preferably with the greatest contrast of line on the whitest possible background. This machine may also produce copies on photosensitive transfer sheets.

Photodrafting film: A translucent, photosensitive, dimensionally stable, polyester film, such as DuPont "Cronaflex," available with matte finish on one or both sides. Matte finish is necessary for pencil or ink drafting and should generally be on both sides. The photo image may be removed by a two-step liquid eradicator.

Projection photography: Reproducing the photo image at a smaller or larger size.

Screening: Photographing through a screen to reduce the intensity of the line or image.

Title printer: A machine that quickly produces from microfilm the letters or lettered copy usable for titling.

Transfer lettering: Lettering of various sizes and styles that can be "pressure-transferred" to the drafting paper or film. Only sheets of lettering labeled "heat resistant" must be used; otherwise they may be subject to dislodging if the tracing is passed over the lamp of a whiteprint or blueprint machine.

Transfer sheets: Preprinted sheets of title blocks, lettering copy, or drawings on a transparent film with adhesive back and mounted on a peel-off sheet. The film may thus be transferred by pressure adhesion to drafting paper or film.

Washoff film: A drafting film with photo emulsion that is washed off during the developing process to eliminate nonsensitized residue after printing. This film is more expensive than direct-process film but allows easy eradication of photographic images by dampening the area. then burnishing it with an eraser.

Wet-process whiteprint: A whiteprint produced from a negative by wet processing (similar to a blueprint) to produce a more durable copy than the regular whiteprint.

Whiteprint: A direct-positive, dry-process print exhibiting dark lines (usually purple or black on a white background) produced on a diazo machine using either liquid or anhydrous ammonia for development.

TRANSFERS

Transfer lettering is available in many sizes and styles, can be easily spaced, and is quick to press on. These letters are easier to erase than stylographic ink lettering. The preprinting of transfer sheets with abbreviations, symbols, standard notes, typical titles, north arrows, graphic scales, and simple standard details allows the transferring of an entire sheet or section of a sheet to the drawing with a considerable savings in time when compared with conventional drawing and lettering. Preparing the abbreviations and symbols on separate sheets or sections for the architectural drawings, for the mechanical-electrical drawings, etc., allows these sheets or sections to be placed with the appropriate drawings.

Office standard details on 8½ × 11″ sheets (black-line whiteprints or originals with black line on white opaque paper) can be quickly photocopied directly onto photosensitive transfer sheets, and these in turn can be pressure-transferred to the drawing sheet. Special title blocks can be similarly produced. The transparent film background of these transfers will result in a light haze when reproduced, which will be objectionable to many. Finishing the drawing by *boxing in* the detail or title block with a heavy outline, with the transfer film filling the entire space, can help to minimize this appearance.

For the whiteprinting and blueprinting processes, the transfer may be applied to either the face or the back of the drawing sheet, but the photo process will only record that which is exhibited on the sheet face unless backlighting is used. Transfers applied to the back of the sheet allow additional drawing, notes, and titling to be applied to the face side, and back-side application protects the appliqué from wear and from the possibility of turned corners during the drafting and printing stages. Standard details and other drawings produced by the photocopier must have the originals printed in reverse in order to affix the transfer to the back of the drawing sheet.

SCISSOR-DRAFTING (OR PASTE-ON DRAFTING)

As the name implies, any photographable drawing, manufacturer's catalog illustration, reprint, or photograph may be cut out and pasted in position on the drawing face, with the entire sheet then being photographed to yield the type of reproducible desired. Scissor-drafting is particularly advantageous to the firm doing an amount of repeat work where details can be reused, especially those that require few revisions. All of the transfer methods discussed above may be used, except appliqués on the back side of the sheet.

Generally the basic drawing sheet is preprinted with a black-line border and title block on an opaque white sheet. Applied drawings may be black-line prints on white paper, black-and-white catalog cuts, black-and-white photographs, or transfer prints, as long as all are optimum for photographic purposes. Lettering and additional detailing in pencil or ink may be applied to the drawing face, with the sheet then being photographed (see Figure 7-1). Further additions and revisions can be made on the phototracing.

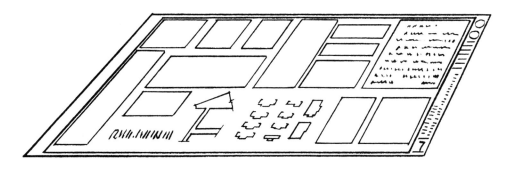

FIGURE 7-1 PASTE-ON SHEET.

The entire scissor-drafting process depends on photography for reproduction, and therefore:

1. All images must appear on the face of the drawings.
2. Images do not have to be translucent, as they do for direct whiteprinting or blueprinting.
3. Pasting marks and other blemishes can be corrected on the negatives.
4. The line photography must be sharp. Variations of shading (such as with pencil poché) will not reproduce well.
5. Shading, patterns, and varying intensities of the final image may be obtained by photographic screening techniques.
6. Photographic reductions or enlargements of a detail may be made prior to pasting on.

Specialized cameras and copiers are available for photoreduction (or even enlargement), thereby allowing images to be reproduced at the desired scale for paste-on or for photocopying. Title printers can instantly produce individual letters or strips of lettering for the titling of plans, details, and sheets.

The process is especially adaptable for typewritten information, such as lengthy notes and schedules, which may be prepared on opaque white paper. The draftor can compose the schedule and write out the information in rough form, draw the division lines after the typing is complete, and paste the copy on the drawing sheet. The secretary can type in all the information, thus avoiding the more laborious hand lettering. Typing is particularly appropriate for structural, mechanical, and electrical schedules, where few symbols are included. A typical typed schedule is shown in Figure 7-2.

PHOTOGRAPHS FOR REMODELINGS AND RESTORATIONS

When working with existing construction, using photographs in lieu of line drawings may frequently save considerable time and be

A	CONCRETE PEDESTAL SCHEDULE						
PED MARK	TYPE	NO. REQ	DIA	TOP ELEVATION	ESTIMATED BOT EL	ESTIMATED LENGTH	DOWELS
P1	B	1	4-0	99-4	92-0	7-4	4-#6x5-0
P2	S	1	5-0	99-4	92-0	7-4	4-#6x5-0
P3	S	1	5-6	99-4	91-0	8-4	4-#6x5-0
P4	B	1	6-0	99-4	90-0	9-4	4-#6x5-0
P5	S	1	6-0	99-4	89-0	10-4	4-#6x5-0
P6	B	1	6-0	99-4	88-0	11-4	4-#6x5-0
P7	S	1	3-0	106-7 3/8	88-0	18-7 3/8	6-#5x5-0

FIGURE 7-2 TYPEWRITTEN SCHEDULE FOR PASTE-ON.

even more descriptive. This technique is especially applicable to remodelings or restorations, for it can economically illustrate the existing conditions in great detail, and the revisions can then be added by note and arrowed to the photographic reproduction. Although the scale may be less than exact, such photographic drawings may be sufficient to adequately describe the conditions of an entire facade of a building or to show the intricacies of equipment and piping in a boiler room. The draftor thus does not spend hours taking on-site dimensions and developing the drawings. Wherever the photographic face can be described in one plane, an appropriate graphic scale should accompany the photograph.

Although the photograph may be applied to the master sheet by the paste-on method, reproducing these on the reverse side of photodrafting film can be advantageous. In this process, the photographs are reproduced in half-tone negatives, and the borders are masked and then rephotographed on the reverse side of the draft-

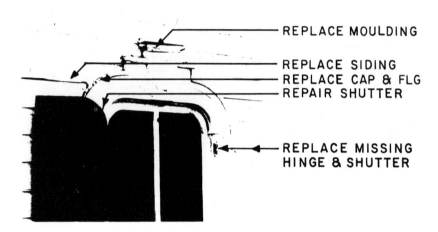

FIGURE 7-3 RESTORATION PHOTO.

ing film. The result is an excellent reproducible sheet that can have additional drawings and notes applied to the face side; the arrows and notes can be applied to the periphery or even to the photo area, preferably in ink (Figure 7-3). A photographic eradicator can remove any unwanted photographic areas. Titles and borders may be applied by hand or by the printing process.

THE OVERLAY SYSTEM

In the overlay system, a basic plan, such as a floor plan or a site plan, is drawn only once (without dimensions, notes, or details) and is photographed on photodrafting film to become the basis for the preparation of overlay drawing sheets on which supplementary information will be drawn and noted by the architect; the structural, mechanical, electrical, and interior consultants; and others. In the process, the basic plan and one or more of these overlays may be photographically combined into a single phototracing for further reproduction purposes.

In order to ensure that the basic film and the overlay will be in perfect registry with each other, a *pin bar* (a metal strip with small protruding studs, available from printers and drafting supply houses) may be taped to each drawing board and the drawing sheets punched to fit precisely over the studs. The printer must also attach a matching pin bar to the photo frame.

Typically, a floor plan is first prepared at accurate scale in black line and photoreproduced on drafting film. Additional film (or film sepia) reproductions are then made for each of the consultants who will be using the plan. The architect retains the original from which whiteprints may also be made. All the other floor-plan-related drawings are then made on other drafting films by overlaying the floor plans. In this manner, overlays may be prepared for (1) architectural dimensions and notes, (2) plumbing, (3) heating and cooling, (4) electrical, (5) reflected ceiling plan, (6) furniture layout, and (7) other floor-plan-related drawings.

The basic plan and column grids may be screened so that they will not appear as intense as the line work and notes of the overlays when they are all photographically combined.

Thus, a combination of the basic plan with two, three, or even more overlays is possible. When photographed they will appear as one composite plan. An overlay for one discipline can be used as an additional base drawing for another discipline, primarily to facilitate coordination between the two. For example, the architectural reflected ceiling grid layout might be included with the printing of the mechanical duct distribution plans, the fire protection sprinkler plans, and the electrical lighting plans. The structural footing and foundation plans might be included with the underground plumbing plans. And the site grading plan might be included with the utility plan.

By the same multiexposure photographic process, sheet borders and title blocks can be made on all or any of the sheets and can be added to or altered as necessary. Such title blocks are photo-

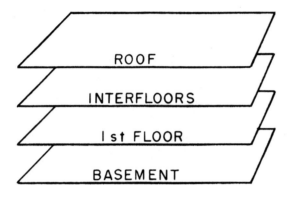

FIGURE 7-4 SHEETS DEVELOPED BY FLOORS.

graphed once, then applied on the standard sheet or stripped onto the sheets as overlays are repeatedly reproduced; the printer may include the various engineering and architectural seals as required on the respective sheets.

Suppose the drawings were being prepared for a building of five floors plus a basement, all reasonably repetitive, as in Figure 7-4. The step-by-step procedure for drawing development might be as follows:

Step 1: A standard-size drawing sheet is laid out with borders, title block, and registry marks, using ink lines and paste-on, then photographed on photodrafting film (prepunched for pin-bar registry).

Step 2: Working from the design-concept drawings, the architect determines the scale to which the floor plan will be drawn and composes it on the drawing face. In concert with the structural engineer, the framing grid and the lines and numbering of the columns are determined and inked on the drawing. This is then photographed on washoff film, producing as many copies as are required by the architect and the engineering consultant for the development of the floor levels and roof plans.

Step 3: The architect develops the most typical floor plan showing perimeter walls with door and window openings, columns, stairs, elevators, mechanical openings, interior partitions, door swings, toilet and mechanical fixtures, and other fixed items. Working over this initial layout, the architect similarly prepares separate sheet layouts for the basement, the other floors, and the roof plan. Exterior and interior dimensions, door numbers, room names and numbers, and ceiling grids are worked out and recorded on reproducible sepias (thus making prints available to the architectural staff and consultants) but are not entered on the tracings at this time, for these dimensions, numbers, and grids would interfere with the consultants' use of the photocopies of these basic plans.

Step 4: Reproductions of the basic floor plans are supplied to the structural, mechanical, and electrical engineers, who develop their working drawings on overlay sheets. Additional floor-plan reproductions are made available to the interior consultant, the phone company, and others who need to coordinate their work.

Step 5: The architect further develops each plan by making revisions, finalizing the interior layout, adding exterior and interior dimensions, room names and numbers, door numbers, and otherwise proceeding to complete the working drawings with hatching of materials, adding of notes, etc. Mechanical and electrical consultants add room numbers (room names are generally unnecessary) to their sheets, positioning them to avoid conflict with light fixtures, registers, etc.

Step 6: Architect and consultants photographically combine the base sheet (or screened base sheet) with each series of overlays to produce the required composite drawings.

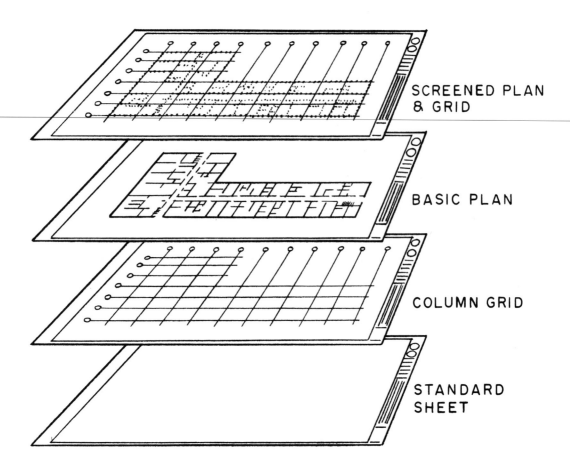

FIGURE 7-5   PROGRESSIVE SHEET DEVELOPMENT.

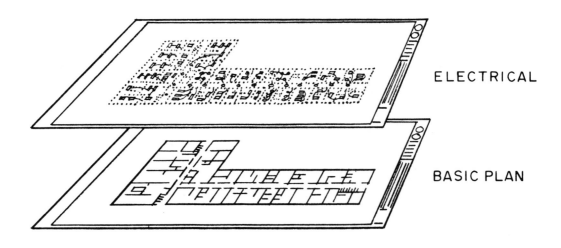

FIGURE 7-6   OVERLAY DEVELOPMENT FROM BASIC PLAN.

Concurrently with steps 3 through 6: The development of other detail sheets and schedules is made by the architect and the consultants using scissor-drafting, projection photography, and transfers, all of which is then photographed onto drafting film, with the drawing then completed by hand drawings and notes.

The resulting combinations of basic plans and overlays required for the final photo-composite tracings are so complex that a "tracing key" system is mandatory. Whether this key system is incorporated in the drawing margin or appears as a master index, or both, the system must be available to and well understood by the draftors and the printer.

Check prints are necessary during the production process. Multiple overlays can be combined with rubber grommets in the prepunched registration holes to hold the tracings together while passing through the whiteprint machine. An amount of slippage can be expected as the tracings pass over the light cylinder, but prints satisfactory for in-house use can be made in this manner from four or five tracings. A better method is to expose the prints in a flat light frame and then develop them in the ammonia section of the whiteprint machine. Although light frames are not inexpensive, they can eliminate many trips to the printer and much of the resulting delay-time.

As with all drawing systems, changes and corrections are inevitable. When the basic plan is affected, the architect makes the change only once and gives each consultant a new reproducible, thereby ensuring that the change is made (the consultant is responsible to make the corresponding changes in the work thereby affected).

The consultants are the major beneficiaries of the overlay system in terms of drafting-time savings, since they are relieved of drawing the architectural line work and of making many of the changes to the basic plans. More of the photodrawings are produced for their purposes than for the purposes of the architect. Therefore, the consultants as well as the architect have much to benefit from the overlay system, and all must coordinate and cooperate to ensure its success. Tacit approval of any system will not make it work; only a strict adherence to the system will develop its potentials.

THE PHOTOGRAPHIC PROCESSES

The mechanics of the photo processes depend largely on the availability of a well-equipped reproduction shop with horizontal cameras, a backlighted vacuum frame, and darkroom facilities. Each office might prefer to have its own equipment, but few can afford it and few could operate it effectively. The work done by the reproduction shop will be expensive and must be evaluated against the savings made by eliminating repetitive drafting. Both the architect and the consultants should be involved in the decision making, for they should each share appropriately in the resulting costs and in the benefits.

In the process of making photographic reproductions from any of the techniques described, several options are available to the architect and the printer, each with a different quality and cost. A conference between the architect and the printer to determine the most adaptable processes and techniques will be most effective at the very outset, before any drawings have begun. A working knowledge of the printer's requirements is imperative if a smooth flow of quality drawings from production through reproduction is to be maintained and done so at an economical price.

In the process of making photographic reproductions on drafting film, the drawing masters (tracings or paste-ons) are supplied to the printer, who can make a full-size negative on which the edges of the paste-on and other blemishes are obliterated by opaquing. This negative is then reproduced as a drafting-film positive, with the printing being made on the back side in order to permit drawing and heavy erasures on the face side. All opaque paste-ons must be on the face side of the drawings, and all transfers must also be on the face side unless backlighting photography is available. Using ink rather than pencil on the original will improve the photo image.

Any plan or detail (the whole sheet or any part of it) may be screened, and any arrangement of basic sheet and overlays may be combined photographically to produce a single composite sheet with the screened areas appearing subordinate to the full-strength line work and lettering.

As an alternative process where time is of the essence, or for other uses where blemishes are not as important, a direct-positive film may be produced, thereby circumventing the negative-producing process.

A second alternative is to reduce the master sheet to an 8½ × 11″ or even smaller negative by a projection camera. The resulting negative is opaqued and then reprojected to its original size to make a drafting-film positive from which further prints may be reproduced. This process is more economical than the full-size negative process, above, in that the initial reduction eliminates or reduces many of the blemishes, and thus the opaquing time is considerably reduced. The quality may be slightly inferior to that of the first process, but in many instances the finished reproduction will be entirely satisfactory.

A third alternative is to make each reproduction a negative from which wet-process whiteprints can be reproduced.

In the choice of processes, the methods whereby future revisions will be made should be considered. Those processes using negatives require the negative to be revised before new positives can be made.

OFFSET PRINTING

Using the same basic preparation and photographic techniques, a full-size negative is converted to plates for the offset press. This method provides high-quality reproduction and the availability of more than one color in the reproduction process. For example, a screened basic plan might be run in light blue with the electrical overlay printed in red and the mechanical overlay in green. The only limitations are that each color separation requires a separate plate, and readability may suffer when several colors make the drawing "too busy."

Whether this type of reproduction method is chosen usually depends on the number of copies required. Where the cost break occurs is somewhat speculative, but probably the offset methods become feasible when 100 or more sets of documents are necessary; for large quantities the multicolor runs may not add substantially to the expense.

A result similar to that of the two-color run can be made with one color when the base sheet is lightly screened and the overlay sheet contains details, lines, and lettering at full strength, and the two are made into a single composite sheet before being converted to the offset plate. A strong contrast in two tones of a single color (such as blue/purple) aids the readability.

REPRODUCTIONS AT REDUCED SIZE

Occasionally the reproduction of drawings at a reduced size is advisable, or may even be required by certain governmental agencies or certain owners. The advantages of a 50 percent reduction of a 24 × 36" set of drawings (to 12 × 18") are apparent in terms of storing, handling, packaging, and mailing during the bidding and construction period. The mailing, handling, and packaging charges can result in savings with any quantity, but whether the cost of reduced-size reproduction is a factor *depends* on the quantity. There are disadvantages in that builders prefer large-scale drawings for improved accuracy in estimating, and several sets of the large-scale drawings will probably be necessary anyway for the builder's superintendent during the construction; moreover, the preparation of drawings for reduced-size reproduction requires some additional care by the draftors. The U.S. Corps of Engineers requires the use of reduced-size reproductions and sets forth specific requirements for the drawing preparation.

Drawing the sheet at a scale exactly double the final document size may be particularly helpful when drawing for reduction. This improves the accuracy in scaling, because $1/8''$ scale then becomes $1/16''$, etc.

When a large quantity of reproductions is necessary, the reduced-size offset reproduction system may become especially economical, and reproduction in colors may then be at little more cost than for black-and-white.

For small quantities, there are direct-reduction copy machines that can make a reduced-size copy of a drawing without other photo or printing processes. Sheets as large as $36 \times 24''$ can thus be instantly reduced as much as 50 percent.

ADDITIONAL POSSIBILITIES

The development of site plans is another prime candidate for the overlay process in that the basic plan illustrating the buildings, streets, parking areas, and other physical elements can be produced as a screened layout and supplemented by overlay sheets containing the disciplines of landscaping, and mechanical, electrical, and civil engineering. For housing or apartment projects where basic plans are repeated, the original architectural floor plans can be photographically reduced to the scale of the site plan and scissor-drafted to make up the composite site drawing.

For many small projects, it may be convenient and economical to include specifications on the drawing sheets. The equivalent of 12 sheets of normal specifications can be placed on one $24 \times 36''$ sheet by typing on white paper and pasting on, then photographing on drafting paper or drafting film. Thus, only a few drawing-size sheets are necessary to include a sizable set of specifications.

When the sheets are to be reduced in size through reproduction, the use of pica or larger type will usually permit a 50 percent reduction with reasonable clarity.

The photodrafting process is in its infancy. Many techniques are certain to be discovered and developed which will offer additional options for the production of working drawings.

8

REFERENCES, CONSULTANTS, AND CHECKLISTS

REFERENCES, CONSULTANTS, AND CHECKLISTS

In an era of increasing complexities in building requirements and of increasing demands for professional competence, the architectural staff must have available the reliable expertise of others. This should begin with a library of familiar books to which the staff members may refer and extend to professional consultants who can assist in the planning and detailing of the specialized building systems. To assist in coordinating the many functions of the production period of the working drawings, a series of reliable checklists is also an invaluable aid.

REFERENCE MATERIALS

The policy will vary from office to office as to which reference materials are to be required and which are preferred and who will furnish them—the office or the employee. Whatever the policy, having adequate and appropriate reference materials always at hand and having personnel thoroughly familiar with them are essential for competence and efficiency.

Codes and Regulations

Since buildings must conform to codes, regulations, and ordinances, these reference materials should be readily available and regularly consulted. Every draftor should be thoroughly familiar with these documents, which exercise a large measure of control over the building design and the drawings. Documents with which personnel are familiar should include, at least, the applicable building code(s), the Life Safety Code, the local zoning regulations, the provisions for the handicapped, and the fire-resistance ratings of materials and assemblies.

Reference Books and Manuals

These technical books may be of help to the draftor:

Applied Structural Design of Buildings, T. H. McKaig, McGraw-Hill Information Systems Company, New York, 1965.

Architectural Graphic Standards, 6th ed., C. G. Ramsey and H. R. Sleeper, John Wiley & Sons, Inc., New York, 1970.

Architectural Metal Handbook, National Association of Ornamental Metal Manufacturers, Washington, D.C.

CRSI Handbook, Concrete Reinforcing Steel Institute, Chicago.

Home Wiring Handbook, Westinghouse Electric Corp., Pittsburgh.

HUD Minimum Property Standards, One and Two Family Dwellings, U.S. Department of Housing and Urban Development, Washington, D.C.

Manual of Acceptable Practices to the HUD Minimum Property Standards, U.S. Department of Housing and Urban Development, Washington, D.C.

Manual of Lathing and Plastering, Diehl, MAC Publishers Association, New York.

Manual of Steel Construction, American Institute of Steel Construction, Inc., New York.

National Plumbing Code Handbook, Manas, McGraw-Hill Book Company, New York, 1957.

Simplified Site Engineering for Architects and Builders, H. Parker and W. MacGuire, John Wiley & Sons, Inc., New York, 1954.

Specifications for Structural Concrete for Buildings, American Concrete Institute, Detroit.

Standard Grading Rules for West Coast Lumber, West Coast Lumber Inspection Bureau, Portland, Ore.

Timber Construction Standards, American Institute of Timber Construction, Washington, D.C.

Webster's New Collegiate Dictionary, G & C. Merriam Company, Springfield, Mass.

WoodBook, Wood Products Publications, Tacoma, Wash., 1958.

Through the experiences of the principals and the staff, many construction techniques will have been used and found to be acceptable—or found to be less than best. Time-saving methods for stair layout, for example, may have been devised, or standards for automobile parking diagrammed. Someone may have researched the causes of condensation or the fundamentals of thermal movement in buildings. None of these "thought projects" should be laid aside; they should be converted to tables, diagrams, or dissertations and made available to the design staff in ready-reference handbook form. This handbook should not only describe or illustrate the preferred method, it should *explain the purpose and the theories involved*. Table 8-1 describes a minimum list of design and construction items that should be included in this "construction data handbook" of the office.

In addition, offices that specialize in certain building types, such as residences, hospitals, religious buildings, etc., may find it convenient to maintain a booklet of most often used products, thereby saving time when searching for the frequently referred-to materials.

Samples of Materials

Each office should maintain samples of those materials often required for reference in detailing and product selection. To be able to see and touch these materials is important in the process of selection. In addition to the normal assemblage of carpets, tiles, ceiling panels, etc., samples of the following items will frequently be of benefit to the draftors:

Set of sheet-metal plates marked by gauges for copper, aluminum, and galvanized and stainless steel

Display of nails, bolts, toggles, screws, and expansion anchors

Panels of finished and unfinished woods and plywoods

Sections of metal and wood door and window frames

Sections of drywall and plaster-edge moldings

Sections of ceiling grid systems, channels, and other suspension devices

WORKING WITH CONSULTANTS

The efficient preparation of working drawings requires clear communication and cooperative coordination between the architectural staff and the consultants whether the consultants are in-house or are serving by contract to the architect.

Communications

By the time the design development phase has been completed, many decisions have been made by the architect and the consultants and have been recorded in numerous notes and other communications. As the project advances into the working drawings phase, all these decisions and agreements, along with further directions, should be formalized in a memorandum issued to each consultant. Each office will develop its own format for these memorandums, but the following examples will indicate a general outline of the information that needs to be communicated. Each memorandum to consultant should include the general requirements of the project, among them:

1. The budgeted cost of construction for those elements under the control of the consultant

2. The responsibility to keep aware of the budgeted estimate and to notify the architect of any changes required in the budget

3. The method by which the construction will be bid and built: by single contract, multiple contract, Fast-Track, or other

4. The progress and completion schedule, including due dates for delivering progress check sets of drawings and specifications and for delivering final working drawings and specifications

5. The drawing-sheet size, bordering, and title block

6. The number and types of copies of specifications required

7. The conformance of the drawings and specification formats with the architectural systems

TABLE 8-1 Table of Contents for a "Construction Data Handbook"

Expansion and contraction allowances	Vapor barriers
Stair design	Hardboard and pegboard
Roof-pitch conversion	Wood and plywood paneling
Expansion anchors	Wood shingle siding and roofing
Thermal insulation	Wood shelving
Condensation control	Wood siding
Sound intensity and reduction	Subgrade wall waterproofing
Floor, ceiling, wall, and partition ratings for fire and sound	Above-grade wall waterproofing
Roof drainage	Sheet-metal selection by material, type, and gauge
Mounting heights for fixtures and equipment	Selection of gutters and drainage conductors
Normal furniture sizes	Metal and fabric flashings
Grade slopes for walks, drives, and parking	Sheet-metal roofing
Foundation drainage	Roof-deck insulations
Storm-water runoff	Membrane roofing and flashings
Paving, curbs, and gutters	Skylights and skydomes
Standard parking layouts	Roof hatches and vents
Driveway entrance layouts	Construction sealant selections
Lawns and plantings	Wood and metal windows
Steel reinforcement bar sizes	Metal doors and doorframes
Temperature reinforcement for concrete	Wood doors and doorframes
Slab on grade reinforcement	Folding, sliding, and upward-acting doors
Joints in concrete	Standard hardware finishes

Hardware selections

Maximum glass sizes

Glazing methods and glazing sealants

Resilient floorings

Terrazzo

Unit sizes for block and brick

Coursing for block and brick

Wall bond beam design

Reinforcement in masonry walls

Construction joints in masonry

Masonry mortars

Structural facing tile sizes/coursing

Stone retaining wall design

Cut stone

Masonry wall insulation

Fireplace design

Steel open-web joists installation

Steel roof-deck installation

Steel stair construction

Framing-lumber sizes and stress grades

Typical wood framing details

Holding power of nails, screws, and framing anchors

Plywood for sheathing roofs, walls, and for subfloors

Glue laminated wood framing

Wood decking

Wood boards and finish

Soffit panels

Wood cabinets

Plastic laminate countertops

Wood floorings

Ceramic tile and quarry tile

Drywall partitions

Suspended ceilings

Paint materials and methods

Acoustic ceilings

Toilet partitions

Showers and shower doors

Retractable partitions

Chalkboards and tackboards

Mailing devices

Fire extinguishers

8. The responsibility for progressively reviewing the consultant's drawings with the developing architectural drawings

9. The preparation of tentative systems and equipment layouts for coordination approval before they are finalized on the drawing sheet

   The memorandum must also include specific instructions for the project, such as:

Heating, Cooling, and Ventilating

1. Designation of rooms and spaces that have been provided for the heating, cooling, and ventilating equipment, and the general understanding of the anticipated equipment in each space

2. Confirmation of equipment and sizes where these have been preliminarily established

3. Type of duct systems anticipated under the floor, in the attic, etc.

Plumbing

1. Agreements with utility companies for service

2. Available site information on utility locations

3. Requirements for specific installations, such as water heating, hydrants, roof drainage, etc.

Electrical

1. Local power company service connection

2. Locations of load centers

3. Specifics on fire-alarm systems, raceways, and other systems

4. General and special types of lighting fixtures required

5. General lighting levels expected, listed by types of spaces; for example: offices, dining, and corridors

6. Requirements for layout coordination with the ceiling grid

Structural

1. Report of soils engineer
2. Confirmation of previously agreed-on types and sizes of structural items, such as open-web steel roof joists, steel decks, thicknesses of framed floor slabs and slabs on grade, etc.
3. Requirements for an early diagram of sizes of columns, beams, and other structural components
4. Other specific instructions

Work by Others

Each memorandum should specifically outline (1) that equipment which is not a part of the contract but which requires service connections and (2) any materials and installations that are furnished by the owner or someone other than the contractor.

Coordination

The architect and the consultant must keep each other advised, by progress drawings and communications, of the developments and changes that will affect the other's work. A written record of each conference and telephone call should be kept; no decision should have to be made twice.

Thoughtful coordination during the Design Development Phase should have led to the discovery of the major points of concern, but additional complications will develop that must be reconciled during the Construction Documents Phase. A beam and a duct may be competing for the same space, a beam may extend below a ceiling, a plumbing pipe may be too large for its partition, the previous oversight of a vertical duct in an important space may cause considerable design change, the coordination of lighting fixtures with ceiling grids may result in differences in opinions, and a late requirement by the owner may necessitate changes by everyone.

The consultant must remain alert to the potential problems and must notify the architect promptly of any discovery that will require a decision. Whatever the reasons, problems must be resolved as promptly as they arise, and it is the responsibility of both the consultant and the architect to coordinate and cooperate with each other to effect proper decisions to the benefit of the project.

In accordance with the progress schedule and in ample time for closeout coordination, the consultant should furnish the architect with a reproduction of the nearly completed drawings and specifications. The consultant should be responsible for these documents being accurate and complete and fully coordinated with the architectural documents. The process of checking and ensuring the accuracy and coordination of all the documents must be a thorough and cooperative effort by the consultant and the architect.

CHECKLISTS

Checklists for Drawings

Checklists are mandatory for thoroughly organizing the preparation of the working drawings. They should be kept available and referred to regularly by the draftors as the working drawings develop. The draftor should not depend on another person for thoroughness. Neither should the draftor or a checker rely on any checklist as being complete, for every project will differ somewhat in the scope and preparation of the drawings.

The checklists in this chapter are presented as suggested formats. Each office can edit the checklists according to its needs. The checklists are divided into the major drawing elements (floor plans, wall sections, etc.) and subdivided under these to include (1) the general requirements defining the scope of the drawing, (2) the items that should normally be indicated by drawing, identified by notation, or dimensioned, (3) the dimensions that will be specifically required, and (4) auxiliary details to accompany and support the drawing. Table 8-2 sets forth a reasonably comprehensive checklist for normal architectural projects and includes brief checklists for the structural, mechanical, and electrical engineering, as a coordinating guide for those disciplines.

Closeout

Several concurrent functions are necessary as the drawings and specifications are brought to a close. During the preparation of the specifications, the writer should be giving the drawings a detailed review, thereby discovering details that need amplification or clarification and errors that need correction. These items should be redmarked on a set of whiteprints for return to the draftors. At the same time, the draftors should be reviewing the drawings against the checklists and finishing everything that has been deferred, including referencing letters and numbers, completing titles and subtitles, bordering details by groups, and completing and correcting all drawings.

The consultants should make a general and concerted review with the architectural staff, comparing and coordinating all elements of the engineering drawings and specifications with the architectural ones.

When the specifications, the architectural drawings, and the consultants' drawings have been largely completed, a proof-copy of the specifications and a set of whiteprints should be made for the checkout.

Checkout

The final checkout of the architectural drawings and specifications is the responsibility of the project architect whether some of the checkout duties are delegated to others or not. Red-marked corrections from the specifications writer's work prints and from any other staff's or consultant's work prints should be transferred to one set of

TABLE 8-2 Checklists for Drawings

SITEWORK

General Requirements

1. Site plan illustrating (a) building plan in relationship to property; (b) site improvements; (c) existing and finish grades
2. Auxiliary details
3. Utilities; on separate mechanical-electrical drawing, except on simplest projects
4. Landscape plan, usually separate from the site plan

Indicate, Identify, Dimension

1. Property lines
2. Adjacent streets, roads, and curbs
3. Easements and building setback lines
4. Structures and items to be removed
5. Existing structures to remain
6. Existing wells, cisterns, and foundations; and their disposal
7. Trees and shrubs to be removed
8. Existing trees to remain
9. New building
10. North arrow
11. Walks, drives, and curb openings
12. Parking areas and paving
13. Retaining walls
14. Patios and terraces
15. Fences
16. Cooling tower and condenser slabs
17. Flagpoles
18. Sewage disposal system
19. Underground tunnels
20. Culverts, drainage ditches, catch basins, and subgrade drains
21. Numbered soil-boring locations
22. Lawn areas
23. Perimeter line indicating extent of sitework, if other than continuing to property line or to streets
24. Bench-mark identification and elevation
25. Architectural floor elevation relationship to site datum, such as

> ARCH FL/EL 100-0
> = SITE EL 961.5

26. Existing and finish contour grades
27. Finish spot grades
28. Utilities, including (a) power lines—with poles if aerial; transformer; (b) telephone lines—with poles if aerial, with manholes if underground; (c) sanitary sewer: size; manholes; flow-line elevations; (d) storm sewers: size; manholes; flow-line elevations; (c) fire hydrants; (f) water lines: size; (g) gas lines: size; (h) site lighting poles and lines

Specifically Dimension

1. Overall of building and its locating dimensions; where site is irregular, indicate parallel or angular relationship of building to property line or other reference
2. Locations and widths of curb openings, drives, pavements, and walks
3. Sizes and locations of other site features

Auxiliary Details

1. Soil-boring log
2. Legend of special site symbols
3. Curbs and gutters
4. Walks and pavings
5. Steps and ramps
6. Railings
7. Fences
8. Retaining walls
9. Planters

Landscaping

1. Site diagram of lawns, trees, plantings, and other landscaping features
2. Identification of sodded and seeded lawns
3. Numbering or abbreviations coordinating landscape elements with descriptions in specifications

FLOOR PLAN(S)

General Requirements

Plan(s) representing a horizontal section through the building at approximately 5'-0" off floor, with reasonable variation to indicate wall openings

Indicate, Identify, Dimension

1. Title, "Floor Plan"; when several levels: "Floor Plan—Level 1," etc.
2. North arrow
3. Column-line identifications
4. Modular-grid indications
5. Axis lines and center lines, where required
6. Wall and partition hatching
7. Notation of wall materials, at least once each plan
8. Types of columns (concrete, steel, etc.)

9. Elevators, dumbwaiters, and escalators
10. Stairs and handrails
11. Duct and riser openings
12. Wall furring
13. Chutes
14. Fireplace
15. Flues and flue liners; cleanouts
16. Toilet partitions and screens
17. Shower stalls
18. Stoops and platforms, with elevations and slopes
19. Belt courses and projections
20. Floor elevations at each change of level
21. Change lines in floor coverings
22. Expansion joints (floors, ceilings, and walls)
23. Floor recesses
24. Floor drains, basins, and sumps
25. Overhanging roof lines and canopies where important (dotted)
26. Room names and numbers
27. Doors, numbers, and swings
28. Door saddles and thresholds
29. Railings
30. Plumbing fixtures (and vent stacks for residential)
31. Interior roof drains
32. Access panels to spaces
33. Radiators and convectors
34. Ceiling beams (dotted)
35. Changes in ceiling levels, unless reflected ceiling plan provided
36. Clothes closet rods and shelves
37. Linen and other storage shelving
38. Section-cutting planes
39. Chalk and tackboards
40. Base cabinets and wall cabinets
41. Fixed seating
42. Athletic court lines
43. Lockers and locker bases
44. Telephone booths
45. Built-in safes
46. Fire extinguishers and hose cabinets
47. Mirrors
48. Built-in refrigerators
49. Other equipment in contract
50. Equipment furnished by others, important for reference (dotted and marked "NIC")

Specifically Dimension
1. Exterior walls and openings
2. Columns
3. Interior partitions and spaces
4. Locations of special features

BASEMENT OR FOUNDATION PLAN

General Requirements
Plan with similar indications, identifications, and dimensioning as floor plans, above, but with these additional indications, as applicable:
1. Wall and floor construction joints
2. Excavated areas
3. Unexcavated and filled areas
4. Areaways and area drains
5. Floor drainage slopes and lines
6. Floor drains, basins, and sumps
7. Boiler and equipment pads
8. Louvers or vents
9. Tunnels and pipe trenches
10. Accesses to tunnel; crawl space; other
11. Perimeter and interior subgrade drains
12. Extent of waterproofing

ROOM FINISH SCHEDULES
Refer to Figure 6-8.

DOOR SCHEDULES
Refer to Figure 6-12.

REFLECTED CEILING PLANS

General Requirements
Reflected plan of grid panels, tiles, and ceiling vaults

Indicate, Identify, Dimension
1. Walls and partitions penetrating ceiling
2. Complete pattern of grids
3. Each change of ceiling level in open spaces
4. Valances, pockets, and other special conditions
5. Identification of each ceiling type by encircled number keyed to accompanying legend

Auxiliary Details
Special grids or patterns, valances, and ceiling drops

ROOF PLAN

General Requirements
Top-view plan indicating roof configurations, wall tops, roof accessories, and equipment on or at roof level

Indicate, Identify, Dimension
1. North arrow
2. Penthouse
3. Equipment enclosures
4. Roof-top heating/cooling equipment

(Continued)

TABLE 8-2   Checklists for Drawings (*Continued*)

5. Towers; television mountings
6. Skylights
7. Hatches
8. Exhaust fans; ventilators; flues; vents
9. Roofing materials
10. Roof drains
11. Ridges, hips, and valleys
12. Roofing expansion joints
13. Parapets; copings; gravel stops
14. Gutters; gutter expansion joints; splash pans
15. Saddles, cants, and flashings
16. Crane anchors

BUILDING SECTIONS (LONGITUDINAL AND CROSS SECTIONS)

General Requirements

1. Simplified small-scale sections that indicate at a glance the general conformity of the structure and leave further explanation to larger details
2. Indication of structural members, leaving size notations and specifics to structural drawings; exception: simplified small buildings or residences may use these sections for more detailed structural indications
3. No indication of finishes and equipment on *far* walls unless necessary for complete communication

Indicate, Identify, Dimension

1. Exterior walls
2. Foundations
3. Subgrade drains
4. Underfill and vapor barrier
5. Slabs on grade

6. Existing grade if below slabs (dotted)
7. Tunnels
8. Grade at exterior walls
9. Columns, piers, and pilasters
10. Floor framing and floor construction
11. Ceilings
12. Roof framing, deck, insulation, and roofing
13. Coping, gutter, cornice, or parapet
14. Penthouse
15. Elevators, chutes, and conveyors
16. Stairs (dotted if beyond partition)
17. Ducts and risers (where important)
18. Doors and windows

Specifically Dimension

1. Floor to floor and roof construction heights, with elevations related to datum
2. Variations in floor levels
3. Floor to suspended ceilings
4. Roof pitches

WALL SECTIONS

General Requirements

1. Sections depicting general wall conditions at scales sufficiently large to diagram construction without confusion; sections full height, from footing to roof, wherever possible
2. Footings, foundation walls, and other structural elements drawn to scale and materials noted; details left to structural drawings; exception: simplest buildings and residences may include structural details

Indicate, Identify, Dimension

1. Wall; foundation; materials
2. Slab on grade, vapor barrier, and underfill
3. Waterproofing and drain
4. Perimeter insulation
5. Floor construction (framing and finishes)
6. Floor connection to wall
7. Roof construction (framing; deck; insulation; roofing)
8. Beams; joists; truss connections
9. Wall and ceiling insulations
10. Interior wall and ceiling finishes
11. Cornice, eave, or coping
12. Soffits and soffit vents
13. Wall and sill flashings; weeps
14. Lintels
15. Masonry bond or anchorage
16. Anchor bolts
17. Roof pitch

Specifically Dimension

1. Wall thickness
2. Vertical strings for (*a*) floor to floor and floor to roof construction; (*b*) number of courses, if masonry (bed-to-bed joints); (*c*) heights of sills, projections, and openings from floor or start of coursing
3. Width of overhang
4. Cornice; coping
5. Datum reference elevations tor floors, roof slabs, and other levels

EXTERIOR ELEVATIONS

General Requirements

Drawing of the vertical building walls, illustrating every exposure and the vertical dimensions of components

Indicate, Identify, Dimension
1. Wall materials
2. Existing grade line when grade is uneven or complex (dotted)
3. Finish grade line
4. Floor and roof lines
5. Foundations, footings, and areaways (dotted)
6. Stairs and landings, if in areaways or otherwise pertinent (dotted)
7. Windows and doors; identification numbers; vent indications
8. Type and thickness of special glazing, unless scheduled
9. Exposed columns
10. Sills; ledges
11. Parapets; copings; fascia
12. Gutter; expansion joints
13. Scuppers
14. Drainage conductors
15. Splashblocks
16. Flashings
17. Roofing material, if visible; ridges; hips; valleys; saddles
18. Canopies
19. Skylights
20. Roof vents, flues, and hatches
21. Louvers, fans, and ventilators
22. Railings
23. Ladders
24. Wall expansion joints
25. Signs; lettering
26. Section-cutting planes
27. Title each elevation by facing direction; "West Elevation," etc.

Specifically Dimension
1. Floor to floor and floor to roof

heights, including elevations related to datum (finish floors and roof slab for concrete-framed; subfloors and top of wall plate for wood-framed; finish floors and top of roof framing for steel-framed)
2. Masonry shelf elevations related to datum
3. Pitch of sloped roofs
4. Flue heights
5. Lintel heights
6. Parapet and coping heights

STAIR SECTION

General Requirements
1. Vertical floor to floor section illustrating stair and headroom
2. A stair plan immediately below or above the section

Indicate, Identify, Dimension
1. Carriages and structural members, except as included in structural drawings
2. Special nosings and stair coverings
3. Curbs and handrails

Specifically Dimension
1. Floor to floor and floor to landing heights
2. Run; as 13 T @ $10\frac{7}{8}\pm$ = 11-9
3. Rise; as 14 R @ $7\frac{1}{4}$ = 8-5½
4. Height of curb
5. Top of handrail to line of tread nosings

Auxiliary Details
1. Typical tread and riser
2. Handrails and brackets
3. Curbs

INTERIOR ELEVATIONS

General Requirements
Drawing of vertical faces of interior walls and partitions, illustrating materials, configurations, and vertical dimensions of special elements

Indicate, Identify, Dimension
1. Finish wall materials and bases
2. Windows, doors, and openings
3. Special elements

CABINETS, SPECIAL EQUIPMENT AND OTHER DETAILS

General Requirements
Enlarged plans, elevations, and sections with dimensioning as necessary to illustrate the construction

Indicate, Identify, Dimension
1. Materials and installation components
2. Attachments to walls, floors, and ceilings
3. Number of units required, if more than one

Specifically Dimension
1. Height, width, and depth of units, or of the spaces they are to occupy
2. Thicknesses and other sizes of materials and components
3. Counter and shelf heights
4. Other physical dimension necessary to allow for fabrication, transportation, and installation

STRUCTURAL

General Requirements
Plans, sections, details, and sched-

(Continued)

199

TABLE 8-2 Checklists for Drawings (*Continued*)

ules describing the structural systems

Indicate, Identify, Dimension

1. Foundation walls, footings, pedestals; schedules
2. Areaways; retaining walls
3. Floor framing plans; north arrow
4. Roof framing plan
5. Floor and roof beams, trusses, slabs, joists, and other related framing; details; schedules
6. Columns; details; schedules
7. Stair sections and details
8. Wall-framing details; schedules
9. Lintel details; schedules
10. Special conditions and details; schedules
11. Special structures
12. Roof, floor, and foundation load design criteria and limitations

Specifically Dimension

1. Plans and column spacings
2. Floor to floor and floor to roof (and to other levels) framing heights, with elevations related to datum
3. Tops of footings or pedestals, of foundation walls and masonry shelves
4. Bearing levels and working points

Specifically Coordinate with Architectural, Mechanical, and Electrical

1. Drawing and references systems
2. Openings and framing for equipment
3. Related dimensioning

MECHANICAL

General Requirements

Plans, sections, details, and schedules describing the mechanical systems

Indicate, Identify, Dimension

1. Major heating, ventilating, and cooling equipment
2. Ducts—under floor, or in floor, wall, attic, or furred spaces
3. Registers and grilles
4. Controls
5. Minor HVAC equipment, including (*a*) ranges, ovens, and hoods; (*b*) dryers and vents; (*c*) lab hoods and vents; (*d*) toilet exhaust fans and vents; (*e*) other exhausts
6. Plumbing services: gas; water; storm and sanitary sewers
7. Systems, including (*a*) water heating; (*b*) water treatment; (*c*) process piping; (*d*) vacuum, compressed air, and oxygen; (*e*) swimming pools; (*f*) fountains; (*g*) fire fighting; sprinklers; standpipes; (*h*) fuel piping; (*i*) sewage disposal; (*j*) other special systems
8. Plumbing and piping for all systems
9. Pipe insulations
10. Plumbing fixtures, including (*a*) sinks and lavatories; (*b*) floor basins; (*c*) tubs; (*d*) water closets; (*e*) urinals; (*f*) water fountains; (*g*) other
11. Miscellaneous plumbing equipment, including (*a*) wall and yard hydrants; (*b*) sewage ejectors and sump

pumps; (*c*) catch basins; (*d*) roof drainage; (*e*) floor drains; area drains; (*f*) showers; (*g*) garbage disposers; (*h*) dishwashers; (*i*) grease receptors; (*j*) washer supplies and drains; (*k*) other
12. North arrow; all plans

Specifically Coordinate with Architectural, Structural, and Electrical

1. Drawing and reference systems
2. Specifications format
3. Openings and framing required for equipment, pipes, and ducts
4. Space limitations
5. Electrical connections
6. Mounting height of equipment
7. Equipment furnished by others

ELECTRICAL

General Requirements

Plans, sections, details, and schedules describing the electrical systems

Indicate, Identify, and Dimension

1. Service type and location
2. Load center; distribution panels
3. Disconnect and special switches
4. Light fixtures (interior and exterior) with identification numbers correlated with specifications schedule; mounting height, if not at ceiling
5. Switching and circuiting
6. Controls for mechanical and electrical equipment
7. Outlets, including (*a*) wall and

floor; (b) television; (c) telephone; (d) waterproof; (e) clock; (f) range; oven; (g) washer; dryer

8. Equipment, including (a) range; oven; (b) food warmer; (c) dishwasher; (d) refrigerator; (e) range hood; (f) dryer; (g) washer; (h) toilet exhausts

9. Special systems, including (a) fire alarm; (b) smoke detection; (c) intercom; (d) nurse call; (e) sound reinforcement; (f) music; (g) telephone; (h) door bell; (i) television; (j) time clocks; (k) snow melting; (l) electric heating; (m) emergency power; (n) emergency lighting; (o) raceways; (p) automatic door operators; (q) burglar alarm and detection; (r) lightning protection

10. Other necessary electric devices, wiring, equipment, outlets, and systems.

Specifically Coordinate with Architectural, Mechanical, Food Service, and Structural

1. Drawings and reference system
2. Specifications format
3. Ceiling grid layout
4. Space limitations
5. Fixture and equipment selections
6. Lighting levels
7. Mounting height of fixtures and equipment
8. Exposed conduit locations
9. Connections required by equipment furnished by others

checkout whiteprints. Items requiring correction or completion should be red-marked on this set as the checkout proceeds. On making the corrections, the draftor should cross out the red-marked notations with a transparent yellow marker; in turn, the project architect should spot-check to see whether these final corrections were actually made. Likewise, the specifications should be marked for correction and returned to the specifications writer.

The draftors should not interrupt the checker during the checkout study to borrow marked-up sheets in order to keep up with the corrections. The corrections can wait; concentration is the important concern. Throughout the checkout, the corrections should be marked on *one, and only one,* reproduced set of complete drawings and specifications.

A thorough and coordinated checkout requires an overall review of the drawings and specifications followed by an in-depth evaluation of the details, a comparison of details to plans, a comparison of architectural drawings to engineering drawings, etc. After the general review, there should be a methodical checkout, which can be facilitated by proceeding in the order suggested below. Carefully reviewing schedules and details first ensures that they are well in mind before the review of the more composite elements, such as floor plans and elevations, takes place.

1. Reference system
2. Room-finish schedules
3. Reflected ceiling plans
4. Interior details
5. Interior wall elevations
6. Door schedule and details
7. Building cross sections
8. Wall sections
9. Window details

10. Stair details

11. Floor plans

12. Exterior elevations

13. Site details

14. Site plan

15. Structural drawings with architectural

16. Mechanical and electrical drawings with architectural and structural

17. Key dimensions

18. Final overview and application of seals

In the inevitable chaos resulting from the pressures of finalizing and issuing the project for bids or negotiations, a systematic and thorough checkout must have every priority; otherwise, the chaos will continue throughout the construction period.

INDEX